A Sacred Walk

A Contemporary Perspective of the Medicine Wheel for Everyday Living

---

A JOURNEY TO YOUR TRUE SELF

Carla Goddard, Msc.D.

Tapestry Living Teaching Series

Crystal Springs, FL

Table of Contents

INTRODUCTION

May this journey draw you nearer to the Divine Spirit within and into the ancient teachings of the Medicine Wheel.

The journey of our lives can be filled with twists and turns, but as I have always said, the magic is in the journey. It is through trials that I have found the treasures. I have found the miracles.

Many say that they see courage and strength in my journey, some vigilance and fortitude, others incredible faith and miracles. I see it as a simple journey. When people speak of the miracles performed by Jesus, such as the blind man can now see, the cripple can now walk, and the leper is now healed those are not just some stories in a book. They are my miracles. Those are the miracles that the Divine Spirit has manifested on this journey.

There were times when I was a cripple; unable to stand, walk or even do the simple everyday things that most take for granted like determining when I had to use the bathroom. There have been times in my life when I have had a seizure in the middle of room full of people and came to with EMT's standing over me; people gawking and staring not daring to get to close. There have been times when doctors have said the words "we don't know if she will make it through the night".

I have sat in an IVP clinic for hours while doctors filled my veins with fluid, knowing the drugs they pumped into me might not work. I have lain in bed only to get up and have my hair remain on the pillow along with my tears. I have had times of looking in the mirror and not know who the person looking back was. Wondering where I went? I've been there. I have had my heart stop. I have seen the light that many have spoken of.

I have curled up in a ball and sobbed uncontrollably when I heard the words "your baby didn't make it". Felt the helplessness when your child has been kidnapped. And all you want in the world at that very moment is to hold your baby.

I have walked the city streets and stood on the corner waiting; willing to do whatever was necessary to get that next fix. I have been to the gates of hell and fell through. I have felt the viciousness of being raped. Of having your dignity and innocence stripped from you. I have felt the blade of a knife against my throat. I have felt desperation. I walked the journey where desperation gave way to hopelessness. Thinking the only way out was to relieve the pressure of living. I know where the depths of hell are. I've been there.

I have been to the place where it no longer hurts because you no longer feel ... until you come to.

Looking back I don't see the things others see. I know when you have walked a mile in another's shoes it is only then can you know where they come from and begin to understand them. The journey continues and every day is a miracle. It happens when I awaken. Every day I roll from bed and hit my knees and say thank you to whoever is listening. Every day I notice which flowers have bloomed and take the time to say thank you. Every day I see my children that still live at home and say thank you. Every day I pray for the ones that are not in arms reach and say thank you. Every day I spend time alone with my Divine Spirit and say thank you and please continue to help me. Every day I tell at least one friend how much I love them and appreciate them in my life. Every day I touch the tree of life and inhale its beauty from the roots that delve deep into the darkness of the Earth all the way up to the branches that reach for the heavens. I do this not because of faith. I do this because every day is a miracle.

During this journey into the darkness, the shadows of life, I continued one single daily practice. I humbly, on my knees, asked for something to change, something to give me a way out. I was not even sure many days if anyone was listening; yet, the pure and humble prayer was answered. My teach ability in life was open. When your heart and soul is teachable, when you ask to be shown, the teachers will cross your path. The right book, the right video, the right soulversation (those conversations soul to soul) will come into your life. Perhaps that is why this book has found its way to you.

So I suppose I have walked a journey that some may say shows courage and strength, hope and dreams, faith and belief. But I say I have walked a journey of miracles; as I walked through fear and weakness, hopelessness and desperation, loneliness and discontent. The miracle being that I am walking, I am seeing, and I am breathing life.

- Do I have faith? Yes, but surely is not the same as yours.
- Do I have beliefs? Yes, but surely not the same as yours.
- Do I have dreams? Yes, but surely not the same as yours.
- Do I have hope? Yes, but surely not the same as yours.
- Do I have courage? Yes, because I still can have fear.
- Do I have strength? Yes, because I can still be weak.

So my wish for you is that you have some fear and weakness. My wish for you is that you have your own hopes and dreams. My wish for you is that you find your own faith and belief's. But if along the way you need some love, come find me because I might need some love too. And if you need to cry, come find me because I might need to cry too. If your lonely and need a friend, come find me because I was once alone too. If you want to laugh, come find me because I laugh now too. If you want to sing and celebrate, come find me because today I sing and celebrate too.

It is my simple journey. A tapestry of life that weaves the fabric of my life together one thread at a time.

Many have asked along this journey how I came to find the ancient teachings of the Medicine Wheel. Let me first share that the teachings of the Medicine Wheel are to lead you down a path to a specific location. That specific location is the Cauldron of your Soul. The place where the Eternal Flame of Love exists within us all; it exists whether we can see it, feel it, or even believe it. The teachings share a multitude of paths that can be experienced for you to find that location.

Your journey may be different than mine. Your journey is just that your journey. The teachings, the ceremonies, and the ritual exercises that follow are here for you to find a starting point into the journey to your Inner Temple where the cauldron of your soul awaits. May the ancient teachings come to find a practical application in your daily walk so that you too can experience the wisdom found within the Medicine Wheel.

CHAPTER 1

THE BEGINNING

Medicine Wheel - Even the term seems to invoke a deep primal knowing of what is sacred. Medicine here refers to the teaching of being in harmony and balance with self, with others, with the world around you, and with Spirit. Wheel simply reflects the form of the teaching in a circle. All of life is a circle. Our seasons, our days, our years, and our lives are cyclic.

A wheel or circle has no stopping or starting point. Nothing on the wheel is of greater or lesser value than anything else on the wheel. Think of the Zodiac, think of King Arthur's Round Table – circles are about unity and balance. The Wheel teaches us our connections rather than our differences. The Medicine Wheel teachings at their essence, even among traditions, share core spiritual principles which give a map of how to live. If you are seeking alignment, harmony and to live in cooperation with the universe; the Medicine Wheel can guide you.

While many of the teachings within this book are ancient, old ways of living, they form a simple pattern for life that can be applied even in our contemporary world. We may not have the opportunity nowadays to go out into the wilderness on a month long vision quest to discover our purpose. But that's okay. The teachings of the Medicine Wheel allow us to discover our purpose within ourselves, rather than the exterior world. These ancient teachings still holds truth within them.

Within these teachings we discover how to place technology into balanced context, how to resolve conflict without war, how to defuse anger with space for compassion, and how to dissolve prejudices to allow creativity. The Medicine Wheel teaches us to find our own sacredness within so that when our journey through life becomes tiring, frustrating, or seemingly impossible we can see clearly the beauty that surrounds us. The Medicine Wheel can be our compass in life. When we feel lost, it can be a beacon to guide us back to our center. The deeper within the medicine we go, the more we discover what there is to learn.

The Medicine Wheel is our anchor so that we do not become lost in the fragmented world of technology and off kilter as we are surrounded by imbalance. For example…. It is through the simplicity of breath, the simplicity of song, dance, and stories that we engage with the teachings. Wisdom is knowledge that is applied in daily practice. In the contemporary world we are constantly barraged by exterior distractions and disturbances. We can't ride a taxi without being talked to by a screen. We can't have a conversation with a friend without being interrupted by texts on our iPhones. This is the world we live in, but there is something that can provide balance, and help us return to ourselves. The Medicine Wheel teaches us to pause, listen, and engage with self, with Mother Earth, and with Spirit so that we may return to our inner selves to find what we seek.

How often do we see a canvas painted across the sky at sunset and not even pause to see the beauty? When is the last time you watched the stars light up the skies in a dazzling display simply for the pure joy and awe that it brings? Isn't it easy to offer a simple smile when we pass someone who looks hopeless? What can we learn from the bird who is soaring across the sky in dance or the salmon who swims the river with courageous perseverance? As we journey the Medicine Wheel, we remember the compass that can guide us back to our origins.

The knowledge conveyed by the Medicine Wheel teachings can be applied in life to give us the wisdom to live as authentic, balanced, and joyous souls. The teachings can help us find balance in our homes, our communities, and our entire global world. They can help us meet the needs of Mother Earth, supporting and nurturing her, so that she will continue to sustain us for seven generations to come. The teachings are the story of all life, all creation and the inter-relatedness of everything. The way we live life, the way we act, the way we think, all comes back to the relationship we have with self. Our beliefs and principles, the very code by which we live, determines the way we live. Pausing to reflect upon the cycles of life, the very spokes of life, gives us the opportunity to develop a deeper, meaningful relationship with self and with all of life.

SIX WAYS TO DEEPEN YOUR RELATIONSHIP WITH SELF

1. Respect. The way we treat ourselves is reflected in the way we treat all of life. If we have respect for ourselves, then we respect Mother Earth and all creatures upon her sacred lands.
2. Spirit. The relationship we have with Spirit, the Creator, the Divine Cosmos, or whatever words you give to it, determines our relationship with other beings we walk with.
3. Honesty. Being able to see ourselves honestly allows us to interact with integrity with anyone we encounter. It removes the mask of illusions we all pick up on our journey.
4. Responsibility. By pausing to reflect upon ourselves, we can begin to take responsibility for our actions, and their consequences, and create the life we desire to live.
5. Cooperation. When we see ourselves in an honest manner, knowing both our

shadows and our light, we can work with others to co-create the world in a kind and compassionate way and leaving competition aside. Cooperation allows us to understand that a great gift comes from working in concert with others.

6. Compassion. When we learn our own shadows, we begin to have compassion for others who are not yet able to see their shadows. We can gentle and loving towards the when they seem to offend or hurt us (including ourselves).

A contemporary perspective of the Medicine Wheel journey is one that will allow you to dive into your own inner wellspring and discover your truth. Your beliefs. The Medicine Wheel is not going to tell you what to believe, only where to look. By answering the questions, "Who am I? Why am I here? And, where am I going?" you discover your own answers – your own wisdom. This discovery is the medicine.

What this book offers is not a traditional teaching. The Medicine Wheel you will travel with this book is not of any specific lineage, nor is it simply a shamanic teaching. It is a journey on which spirit has taken me over the years. I share it from my perspective as a woman who has had the immense blessing of learning from many teachers on various paths. Of course it is linked to many traditional paths that incorporate the physical, mental, emotional and spiritual layers of life into a single whole that represents the wellness of a person. I hope to share the Medicine Wheel as it has evolved for me each time I have walked the spokes. You may find, as I did, that what it teaches you is exactly what you need to learn at that moment.

CHAPTER 2

THE INVITATION

I invite you along to travel the journey with me. Make it your own. As you read this book, incorporate what resonates with you and leave the rest. Allow the journey to be what it is. There is no right or wrong way, only *a way*.

Once, I was asked a simple question. This "How is your fire?" I was a bit confused by the question as fire to me was an external element. I did not understand the internal fire that is the center of spirit.

The question was followed immediately by a second question: "If you were to set the intention to heal the warrior spirit within, where would you begin? Would you begin in the North East to understand the warrior energy? The South East to heal? The West to accept the strength? The East where all things begin? Where would you begin?"

I came to the conclusion that to begin a journey, one must take the first step. This is where many are coming face to face with their first block. Setting the intention to simply begin can seem overwhelming. So what did that question mean, about where I would sit in the lodge? The journey will change depending which seat you sit in within the spirit lodge. For example, if you sit in a spirit lodge that faces northwest, and choose the seat on the western side of the lodge, you will find yourself with a great learning about ego.

When I was first asked those questions, I did not know where I needed to sit within the lodge, and you probably don't either. With this book, you can discover your path.

Each journey you take will reveal itself to you, and will emphasize the important fact that all people, all paths, and all things are interdependent and interrelated. Each of us is related to and depends upon one another for existence, for balance, and for wholeness. In this book, you will not find traditional stories to convey the message of each spoke of the Medicine Wheel, but rather personal experiences, personal stories, and personal journeys as they have revealed themselves to me. I will also make suggestions and prompt you with questions to ask yourself as you spend time reflecting upon the journey. Each question you answer will reveal more questions to ask yourself.

There are various sections within the book. They are organized according to the parts of the wheel: the outer spokes, the inner spokes, the center hub, and the mysterious void. The outer spokes are our relations with the world around us – the "middle world" that we live in, our everyday reality. The inner spokes are our relations with self – the lower worlds, our subconscious, or our inner beings. The center hub connects to our relations with ALL including the upper worlds. The Center is our relation with spirit – the Great Mystery.

The worlds of Ordinary Reality (what you see and hear and understand that most people agree upon) and Non-Ordinary Reality (what the shamans and mystics and awakened ones know to be real) are entwined in the soul. We live in this Universe which is very much like a melting pot of people and ideas – some are based in the ordinary reality while others are based in the non-ordinary reality. In order to discover the unification of both realities it is necessary to release what is blocking us. When we release those blocks, the illusion that is held disappears as well. It is when we let go; we can begin to enjoy what we have and all that we desire. There are many paths one can take to let go. These paths are like having a map that explains many of our trials in life that helps us understand our own growth. The Medicine Wheel is a compass to follow on the path to discovery.

In each section of the book, you will find a general description of the direction being focused on, specific questions to ask yourself as they relate to the direction, personal stories and reflections on the direction, and a ritual or specific action you can do that will assist you in incorporating the medicine of the direction.

A few suggestions:

Do not try to read though like a novel and finish in a day or two. Take the time to truly reflect and contemplate. Allow yourself the gift of being with the medicine. Don't rush it.

Begin a journal. Each section will ask you specific questions relating to the spoke being worked on, a sacred contract, and a journey to further explore your relationship to spirit. Write down your thoughts, additional questions, experiences, and daily confirmations about the spoke you are working upon. Don't structure it, but allow yourself the gift of sharing your journey with yourself. You will thank yourself down the road.

There is no set time limit. Work with the medicine of each spoke as long as it feels right. Go back to spokes where you discover a deeper need. Begin where you begin.

There are some ceremonies and rituals included. Do them or not. Change them. Incorporate them. Make them your own. They only serve as examples of how you may connect with the worlds around you.

I am by no means an expert in the teachings and medicine of the wheel; there is always more to learn. The only truth I have come to find is that the more you learn and incorporate into personal living, the more you realize how little you really do know.

Great Spirit, the Creator of All, we pray to open our hearts, open our souls that we may feel and breathe in the new waves of energy that now flow to us from the Divine Source of All Things.

We pray that as our Mother Earth awakens and a new global world emerges, that you gift us with our own voices to be our own truths.

To the Great Spirits of Skies we pray that healing happens within each of us to prepare for this new journey. A deep healing that releases and purifies the soul from limitation, lack and old belief systems that no longer serve our higher good. We pray that each of us who follows this journey can easily and effortlessly let go of pain and separation, that the Eternal Flames transform us, allowing each one of us to become a beautiful Phoenix rising up from the ashes to an authentic self.

Almighty we pray that you bless us with courage to become fearlessly empowered with your inspiration and passion that we may soar through all spiritual challenges between the worlds as your divine warriors. We pray that you become our bridge of light to our divinity giving us the faith and strength to walk as empowered souls with truth, passion and eternal love.

Spirit of the Skies above, we are filled with gratitude and overflowing love for all the blessings you have bestowed upon us, for all the moments you carried us when we could not walk ourselves, for the moments you radiated love, giving us overflowing joys, and for the moments you transformed our tears into laughter.

We thank you for the beautiful canvas painted across our skies each sunrise and each sunset. We pray that each one reveals a deeper understanding and love for the web of life.

It is within this gratitude; it is within this eternal love, that we ask these things for our journey.

CHAPTER 3

DOING THE PICTURES

The spiritual journey is very much like putting a jigsaw puzzle together. Each piece by itself is beautiful, captivating and yet, confusing. It is only when the pieces come together that the true authentic picture comes into view. Each individual piece reveals only a tiny portion of the picture. Each intricate shape is a picture unto itself, even if we don't quite understand it yet. One piece reveals a perspective that shifts as it is interconnected with another piece. So on our spiritual journey; we begin with pieces of the puzzle, looking at different aspects from different perspectives before putting each piece together to reveal the complete picture.

Regardless of where you are starting from, in order to find a new beginning, a new perspective on the pieces if you will, you must be able to define your beliefs. To be able to assess what our own beliefs are and make shifts in our own belief systems, we must understand what a belief is. A belief is simply something that an individual believes to be true. A wise mentor once said there are three sides to every story; my story, your story, and the truth. But your story is your truth and reveals your beliefs. So of course, our beliefs are personal and will never be exactly the same as other people's beliefs. Does this make your beliefs false? Absolutely not.

Many people are trapped by their beliefs into thinking theirs is the only truth. Therefore, in this scenario, anyone who has a different belief must be wrong. We all know where this thinking can lead. Not to awareness and inner knowing, but to a closed mind and spirit.

Beliefs, in part, come from personal experiences. A prime example is that everyone believes something dropped or shot into the air will fall to the ground. Even before Newton figured out that it was called gravity, people believed this to be true, based on their observations. The arrow shot into the air fell down. The heavy bowl that slips out of the hands carrying it falls and shatters. There was a time when humanity as a whole believed that space exploration would never happen – it was considered impossible based on simple observation – things fall to earth and no one had ever done it. These types of beliefs are ones that are shared by the whole of humanity and are based on observation and experience. Most beliefs are not so clear. They are based on personal experiences and personal perspectives that define who we are. Our beliefs include how we react, who we trust and even what we believe is good or bad for us.

Our beliefs define our values, and what we consider good or bad. Some beliefs may be shared generally, but with room for individual differences. For example, members of a certain religion may believe in the same divine being. Yet, each individual will have a personal image of the divine that is different than others.

Everyone's beliefs are formed over the course of a lifetime of experience. As children we want to be liked, and we emulate people we respect. Perhaps we formulate a belief system that is like that of our family, friends or cultural heroes. We also develop beliefs through repetitive events in our early childhood. This is even more prevalent when a traumatic event transpires in early childhood. If we are beaten as children we may come to believe we are not worthy of love. If we are nurtured and loved during our childhoods, we will learn that we are loveable, worthy people. Our culture and environment have an impact on our beliefs. A child growing up in a superstitious household may grow up believing that spilled salt brings bad luck, and a person who is raised in poverty may believe that life is unfair. Many of these beliefs that are formed in early childhood stay with us for our entire lives.

The term belief is sometimes confused with the term value, but they are different. A value is a statement describing what is important to us. A belief is our mindset. Beliefs are like a pair of glasses through which we look at life. Depending on the glasses we wear, they can actually distort our view, changing the true importance of the information we take in and process. Each belief will have a profound effect on how we behave in any situation. Beliefs influence not only what we do but also what we learn from our experiences. They actually shape and mold our outlook and control our reactions. When people limit their beliefs by allowing them to be rigid and unchangeable, the beliefs themselves can become a mortal enemy. For example, if someone believes people are essentially untrustworthy, imagine how scary life is for that person? They will live in fear and dread. If someone believes people are essentially good, they can be open to experience, and discoveries closed to the first person by their beliefs.

Is it possible to shift these harmful beliefs? Absolutely. We can change the beliefs that cause negative results in our lives. A distinct easy way to check if you are limiting your belief is when you start off with the words, "I can't." Whether or not you can or cannot do something is irrelevant. The simple statement of "I can't" has already led your beliefs and mind set down a negative pathway. When you do this it jeopardizes future success or growth in your life.

It is a good idea to take a deeper look at your own beliefs about life by writing some of them down on paper. As we journey through the spokes, we will look for places where you limit your own beliefs and actually cause yourself to be imprisoned by them. By writing and updating your beliefs on paper through this process, patterns will emerge. You will be able to see the beliefs you hold within that are causing you to have negative results. Most importantly, you will begin to discover that by changing a belief (perspective), change can happen.

When embarking, or even preparing, for a new journey, there is a shifting that takes place. During this shift, the spirit and soul can engage in an internal battle of sort. We battle with our very selves about how to open our minds to new perceptions. In 1997 I was struck with transverse myelitis. It rendered me unable to walk without assistance. It took away the experience and sensation of what most consider normality. It shifted my perspective dramatically. I had to open my mind to new sensations and new practices. When things returned to normal with my physical body, it was an awakening – a remembering of what was within. It is the same with spiritual sight, and having that open perspective. It is a remembering.

When you awaken from sleeping in a darkened room and suddenly walk into the light – you can be temporarily blinded. You cannot see any more than when you were asleep. But you are awake, now, and if you allow your eyes to adjust, they will come into an alignment. A whole new spectrum of vision will appear. Suddenly it will be so crystal clear, seeing beyond the horizon, you not only feel the bright rays of sun, but now you see the rainbow vibrancy.

I remember the words of a teacher who said, "There will come a time when you must be your own torch, for there will be no others around to observe. You must remember to be the fire itself. Learn to be the fire. Do not just observe someone else's fire. One path may appear illuminated brilliantly and the other shrouded in foggy mist where on a prism of light, if you are not the fire within, how will you find your way? To the naked eye it is apparent which path to follow – the brilliant one."

It takes time for your spiritual vision to align itself after leaving a dark place of sleep. If you allow your vision to adjust, you will see clearly the path to take. The winds whisper softly, "Become the fire so that when you walk upon the darkest places they are filled with prisms of rainbow light." As you step into the unknown, transforming with spirit, remembering, it is possible to align with your authentic self by clearing, releasing, and purifying your beliefs and perceptions. Those perceptions will come when a breath of oxygen is received to breathe life into the womb – it is then one sees there is no darkness and no light, only a prism of rainbow colors from the deepest of blacks to the brilliant gold's. Shades of color bleed into one another to form new colors that you have never experienced within before. This is the gift of the journey when we walk the spokes of the Medicine Wheel. Your open mind will bring new perceptions of interconnected beliefs. This will be a new spiritual vision.

The journey along the Medicine Wheel will urge that you to ask yourself some difficult questions; questions that will allow you to assess your spiritual self. Questions that will help you to define your truths discover your meaning and purpose in life, and the source of your spiritual strength. Remember that each piece of your own puzzle will provide you its own vision, which will shift when interlocked with another, and again when interlocked with the next piece, again and again until perceptions change, gradually over time. Many times we cannot see the interdependency until the puzzle is complete. Don't judge the piece; simply allow a new vision of the piece to emerge.

People tend to see reality in a linear manner. Human beings are analytical, competitive in nature and their world tends to be hierarchical. Duality and polarity – positive and negative. The Medicine Wheel is an antidote for this thinking. One of the benefits of walking the spokes of the wheel is the holistic perspective it provides. A perspective that is unified based in a creative energy that is spiritual, cooperative, harmonious and balanced.

We have created our world, our reality, in concert with others. Every act on this planet is an act of coexistence and is set into our collective experience through language. All of the souls within our global family are connected through our acts, by way of language, almost as though they were being played out upon a stage. We set our own scenarios and live within them. Our language is powerful and guides the story that unfolds upon that stage. Sometimes we need, or want, to shift our scenarios and change the way we precede with our "play." But shifting is difficult. One way to shift our stage set and shift our scenario is to travel upon the wheel. The Medicine Wheel will help us understand what new reality a different perspective can create.

As we create our world, within the human family, we encounter many crossroads that force each of us to make choices. If we can understand that our individual actions create the stage upon which the world acts, and that each of us sets the tone for the rest of the world, then we can begin to make shifts, not only for ourselves, but for everyone. There are so many paths and crossroads that involve conflicts, wars, fears, economic insecurity, and competition, is it any wonder that so many feel hopeless upon their own individual stages? There are other paths-- sacred paths that are sustainable, harmonious, loving and full of prosperity. So why is it that so many are creating paths individually that is rooted on the dark side of the mountain?

As human souls we have the ability to transform our world-- our own individual worlds and the global world. When we understand that we are all related, we can see a vision unfolding. It is a vision that emerges from deep within our own souls, a vision of who we can become as individuals within a peaceful and harmonious world. So the question: is how do we give birth to the language that will create this world? How do we learn this new language? This is what we will discover in the chapters that follow.

We must begin by healing our pasts and closing our wounds. Each of us has a history that can create chasms among us and in our relationships with the animal and plant kingdoms and Mother Earth herself. We must heal ourselves and our dysfunctional relationships if we wish to create a new world.

Have you ever wondered about the word "tribe"? Even in our modern world, we need to be connected to our "tribe" to live a healthy, connected, loving and supported life. In our tribe, we can return to knowing that all things are related. In our tribe, we can support one another during the healing and creating processes. As modern people, we have hunkered down for too long, become isolated, and forgotten that the circle of life includes the human soul having relationships with other souls. We have forgotten that when any one of us is affected by old dysfunctional paradigms, we are all affected. If we do not return to unity -- the oneness we were created in -- we will remain in the duality of war, conflict, fear, and hopelessness.

It is not enough to simply create our "tribes". We must connect with them, engaging our minds, our hearts, and our souls. When we engage, we affect the whole circle to which we belong. We can use our voices to speak as one, creating a collective consciousness with our tribe. A true "tribe" is a circle that will become broken if each soul within it does not participate. To protect the tribe, we guide, protect, support, nurture, inspire, and challenge one another. Think of the web of life. It is made of the strands of all of us, and all creation. Imagine it this way: if someone speaks ill of another, or puts herself down, or voices hateful thoughts, that web begins to unravel. In walking the Medicine Wheel, each of us can return to the sacredness and harmony of life. The honor of one is the honor of all, because, to repeat a vital truth: we are all related.

As you journey around the spokes you will be honoring the circle, and thus the "tribe" of all related things. The journey shifts perspective from each direction, allowing for a renewed and envisioned belief pattern to emerge. Our beliefs are the root of our reality, so by revealing that new belief pattern, our souls can transform what is at first only a belief into a whole new scenario, outline or vision. The new scenario gradually changes reality: our own, and in time, the worlds.

Remember that single puzzle piece? The journey begins with seeing that single piece of the puzzle and honoring the picture that is revealed in that single piece. Puzzle piece by puzzle piece, the picture emerges, and we gain the gift of introspection and an awareness of our soul truths.

CHAPTER 4

BECOMING A SALMON

As I sat in the stillness of the morning, I listened to the birds waken and watched the cloudy skies give way to the sun as it peeked over the horizon. I watched inwardly, as the flames of my fire gave way to a vast ocean. The ocean was full of salmon swimming in community as though they were searching for a sign, a path, or perhaps a song.

In this early morning vision, the salmon searched and searched; each one sought a specific entrance to a river. A familiar note seems to call out resonating to each one of them, individually. As each salmon heard its own calling melody, it was taken down a vast river. The river was leading them towards a destination of knowing; yet, the river was only the beginning of the arduous journey as they swam strongly against the current. The calling deepened for each of them until they found an entrance to a stream or creek. This stream they hoped would provide safety, seclusion, and stillness in their journey. Each salmon swam only to find that the creeks were full of large rocks, tree branches and dangerous predators. Many had to leap over obstacles. They never paused; they swam until they found the "place". They never tried to make bargains or deals. They did not bemoan their journey. They refused to see failure as an option. They simply kept going until they arrived at the place they must spawn their eggs to continue the cycle of life.

The really amazing aspect of the salmon's journey is that each generation matures and returns to the same place where they were spawned, each year. They travel the same journey over and over. They know the place that calls with a song to their souls. While the salmon of this world travel to different "places", they find their own homes with seemingly magical precision, time and again. How does the salmon's heroic voyage relate to us? Our journeys are very much the same as the salmon's journey as we seek our spiritual home. We are all in search of the river's entrance from the vast ocean we swim in to begin our journey home. We find the entrance to the river and begin the long swim. Battling the current, we wonder if this is our authentic path. We doubt and question, for we believe at first that once we find the river – our path --, there will no more obstacles or fear. That is not entirely true, so we waver momentarily. *Then we hear the song.*

If we do not continue to swim, we will simply be washed back into the vast ocean to begin again. The river simply provides for our entrance way. It is a gateway to our authentic truth. There are as many rivers as there are salmon; and there as many paths as there are humans. No one path or river is right or wrong. They all have songs. They all lead to authenticity for a specific soul.

There are things we can do to find that "home" place. For one thing, there must be movement. It is vital to *move* not once a week, but daily if we wish to make headway "up" the river. What do I mean by "movement"? For human beings, that movement, which for the salmon is a strong swim against the current, is our daily spiritual practice. Daily spiritual practice is key to movement, but it offers so much more. It provides for the experience of being alive, of seeing the beauty on the river's edge, and of strengthening our spiritual beings. Our daily practice is akin to the strokes we must learn in order to swim to our home place. As we learn and practice the strokes, we experience the sacredness that is life. We discover from the many different strokes (spiritual practices) which ones bring us to the joy and beauty inherent in movement.

Simply being present in the river of life, floating along so to speak, is not enough if we want to participate in a spiritual life. Daily practice of the spiritual "strokes" will help us move along our river. In time, after this active participation, we will realize that it is our daily spiritual practice that *creates the river*. The longer we engage in daily practices, the stronger we become and the more manifest *our river*, or our path, becomes. The practice is our commitment to being present in the journey of the river, and seeking the wholeness of life and our true home. The river is not the end of the journey, though, remember? Just as the salmon travels the river to the creek, we too have to find our tributary. As we discovered the beauty of the river, the joy in its song, we begin to hear a new song and know this is our calling to home. The spiritual strength we found in swimming up the river now fortifies us to make the arduous journey up the creek.

Often we come to think that when we reach a certain stage of spiritual life we will have no further obstacles, no further fears. We think we can just ride the current. Yet, when we first begin up the stream, the obstacles seem larger, the fears more prevalent. This is our spiritual maturity. It is the journey in the stream that reveals what each of us needs to heal, what we need to release, and what we need to pay attention to. We developed strength in the daily spiritual practices of the river, and that strength makes it possible to reveal our true, authentic self, a self that has the faith, fortitude, and commitment to travel to the spawning grounds of life.

At last, after our deeply revealing and strenuous journey, the view comes into sight: our home.

Stillness touched by silence. We pause. We relish. We savor the moment. We spawn our eggs and fulfill this cycle of life. Just as the beauty envelops us, unifies our souls with the source of the creek, we find ourselves in movement once more as the cycle of life is never stagnant.

We move with grace and ease, for now the journey lets us flow with the current, back down the stream and into the river. It is a peaceful respite. But be careful. Complacency can cause us to forget our daily practices and we can find ourselves caught up in the rapids. This ride can be enjoyable but is full of the temptation to grasp hold of everything we pass along the way. So, even as our movement quickens and we return to the vast ocean once more, we must continue our daily spiritual practices for the cycle of life to begin anew.

This is the journey. The path. The calling to find the river that sings and the creek that calls to us. Actively participating in daily spiritual practices is a commitment to self and to our Great Spirit and provides the way to follow the songs that call to us. They strengthen and unify us for what lies ahead. They give us the tools so that no obstacle is insurmountable.

Whether you are just finding the river from the ocean, struggling with the current of the creek or savoring the stillness, may your journey be one of beauty, one of aliveness, one of commitment, and one of love.

We are all in search of solutions and new ways to ascend into a higher state of joy, abundance, and balance. In looking to our past we see the ancient teachings of all people. Those teachings show us that we need to return to the sacred web of life of which we are all a part, to show us the way. The walk around the Medicine Wheel spokes is a look to that past.

The sacred web of life, the Medicine Wheel, is about focusing upon our own awareness and responsibilities. It is about remembering that we are all a part of a whole. A whole circle. Within that circle we learn we must be aware that what we do today affects the generations to come, just as what our ancestors did in the past affects us today. Imagine the world had our predecessors made different choices? If we could go back and ask them to look inside themselves and find the truth of the sacred web of life, things might be different today. We can do that for the generations to come, with thoughtful spiritual practice and an acceptance of the web.

Many years ago I was about to embark upon my first journey around the spokes of the Medicine Wheel, yet I had no idea that was what I was about to step into. No teacher said, "Begin here, this is the East." It was some time after that when the pieces of the puzzle were put together for me by a teacher. The journey was interwoven with stories, sweat lodges, and deep introspection.

Nothing was written. It was taught in what I affectionately call 'soulversations', many of which were around the fire, some through joint journeys, and even some kinesthetic learning. Hours and weeks on end were spent talking, journeying, and sweating on the same aspect of life --, and swimming!

It was not until much later that I discovered the journeys with the sharks were really a part of the Medicine Wheel spokes. It was explained by a teacher like this.

LEARNING TO RIDE A BIKE

When you wish to learn to ride a bike, you start with training wheels. The training wheels balance you while you learn. One day you are ready to balance on your own, and take the training wheels off. Here is where the analogy takes a different turn. One day the bike disappears and you are told you must *become* the bike so that the teacher can ride for a while for the teacher is tired of carrying you on his wheels. Then the day comes when you get the honor of becoming the training wheels for another. A circle of life all its own.

The nature of becoming the training wheel begins with learning to ride the bike. So stories, journeys, and lessons may not make sense in the beginning, yet they will make sense in the future. Trust the process; sometimes the simplest lesson is the most profound of teachers.

As we journey together around the sacred circle of the Medicine Wheel, the Great Spirit ensures that what each one of us needs to learn is revealed. Remember, there are no absolutes – there is no right or wrong experiences – only your experience in the journey.

Journal Exercise:

Write three paragraphs of why you are reading this book and what your intention is. If things get painful, it is important to be able to look back and reflect on why this journey is important to you. So what is it that you really want to gain for yourself in this journey around the wheel?

Does this introduction bring up emotions for you? Fear? Excitement? Give the emotion a voice at this point, in your journal.

CHAPTER 5

WHY WALK THE SPOKES

There are a million paths a person can travel. It is vital to understand that only you can have the clarity to know which journey is right for you. To answer the question which path is right for me, ask what does my soul say? The soul will answer with YOUR truth.

How do you know you will hear that truth when you ask the question? The secret to hearing that truth is…listening. In fact, many don't ask the question, but those who do rarely pause long enough to listen for the answers. When you are walking a path that is part of your soul's journey, knowing it is the right path is something within you. That knowing will fill you with strength, courage and fortitude to take each and every step. Now this does not mean that there will not be fear, obstacles, or sorrow – only that there will be a knowing. Walking an authentic path means that, as you experience life, you will engage each moment to the fullest. To get there you must find your own truth and learn to live it, and the path that is right for you, and learn to walk it.

And that is why you walk the spokes -- to discover your truth and to live it, as your authentic self.

So as we embark upon this journey around the Medicine Wheel, I encourage you to ask yourself, "What does my soul say?" To step upon a path, especially a new one is to take a risk. So at each step: remember to listen to your soul.

Taking a risk. Stepping out of the comfort zone. Courage to stand alone. What if I fail? What if I am rejected or disapproved of? What if someone laughs at me? To take a risk takes courage, and we all face those moments, including me. It is a risk for me to teach my medicine in the way that I do, outside the traditional teachings and using a contemporary perspective. Whether it is changing paths, changing how people see you, or standing up for your own beliefs, these risks require the commitment of the heart and soul. Are you ready for this kind of change? If you are, you *can* walk your own authentic path.

Every woman who ever left a bad marriage took a risk in order to live authentically. Every young person who traveled through India to experience life stepped outside the comfort zone to go on a journey of self-discovery. For some, going to a job interview, asking a girl on a date or even stepping outside takes great courage. Whatever the risk, people are so often compelled to do the "scary thing" to live fully and feel whole.

For me, taking a risk outside my comfort zone to teach my medicine is fueled by a flaming fire. Nothing can quench that fire except taking the leap, no matter how scary it is to do so. What is that flame within? It is the flame of love, and it can empower us to accomplish anything, including stepping out on our own. When your purpose in life becomes to step out, empower yourself, and become a better you, the state of your inner life will shift. The shift occurs when you step into the flow of life, the river, the divine nature that surrounds us all. When that fire begins to burn within you, you are willing to try anything, take that risk, and accomplish things you never dreamed possible. And we are back to our question, "How does your fire burn?"

What does this have to do with the Medicine Wheel walk? The fire within you comes from living a sacred life. The purpose for the journey around the wheel is to discover that sacred life. The risks we take are fueled by a need to bring every relationship we have to a deeper sacred place. Discovering the inter-related nature of those relationships is the journey around the wheel. When living a sacred life, the risk of stepping outside our comfort zone seems insignificant because we seek to live in truth, deeper love, and with integrity. A sacred relationship begins with you. Discovering a relationship with self and with the Spirit within is the central part of the journey.

How will it feel to take responsibility to speak the truth, regardless of the reactions of others? It will be risky, but by walking the spokes of the wheel, the truth about yourself is revealed to you. The result is that first important relationship: the one you have with your own authentic self.

Just as that woman stepped out of the familiar but inauthentic territory of marriage into a new, but unfamiliar life, when you take the first step on your new journey, it will require commitment deep within. Just as the young traveler had to find his way in a foreign land, when you discover your purpose, you will find that it is what aligns you and keeps you balanced, regardless of what outcome is revealed. This is true empowerment; empowerment begins by having a connection with the Divine Spirit.

The connection with the Divine Spirit is the fuel for the fire within. It gives you purpose, and pushes you to live your authentic life. When that happens, the scary feeling of risk seems to melt away because of your faith that the journey is the right one for you.

Journal exercise:

In the first exercise we wrote about why you are here reading this book now and what your

45

intention is. Re-read what you wrote. Now ask yourself these questions:

- What am I willing to risk to find that authentic truth for myself?
- What am I willing to risk having a deeper connection with a Divine Spirit I can't see or touch?
- What will fuel my willingness to face risk?

Knowing what you are willing to risk, how far you will compromise your truths, and what will keep you going is vital.

INTENT

The intent of walking the Medicine Wheel is different for all who take the sacred steps. It is up to you to determine what your personal intent of these sacred steps. Setting your intention can be as simple as you wish or as in depth as you wish.

Intent: We want to return to the Sacred Web of Life

We are all a part of the sacred web of life. The journey is not about focusing upon a figure or a tool, but rather a remembrance that we are all a part of the whole. We are one part of a whole circle and within that circle we become aware that what we do affects generations to come;

conversely, what our ancestors did affect us today.

Intent: We all need to return to sacredness.

The goal is to live in sacredness in our daily lives as sacredness was part and parcel of daily life for our ancestors.

Intent: We all can return to the awareness that the Great Spirit resides within us all.

Regardless of the name you give it, the Great Spirit exists as a consciously alive aspect of self, deserving to be respected and honored. The conscious participation with the Great Spirit is essential as it brings inner unity to create a life of joy, love, abundance, peace and harmony.

Intent: We all need to return to silence.

We must learn to pause and listen to the guidance that is available inside and outside ourselves, and not to our own egos. We are responsible for the reality that we live in. Thus we are responsible for changing that reality as well.

Everything is intent.

Journal exercise:

It is vital to give our "beliefs" a swift kick in the butt to wake up before we step into a ceremony. At this point, take a moment to answer the following questions in your journal.

1. What is sacred to me? Define the word not the things.
2. What is value to me? Define the word not the things.
3. What is tradition to me? Define the word not the things.
4. Am I living according to my definition of sacredness? Values? Tradition?

CHAPTER 6

TRADITION AND CEREMONY

The Medicine Wheel has been used by spiritual traditions for centuries. Every spiritual tradition has its own sacred space, ritual, ceremony, and belief surrounding the wheel. Though many will claim it as their own, there are recordings of wheels and circles being sacred in nearly every spiritual path throughout history. The Hindu mandalas, the circle of Stonehenge, the Zodiac wheel, and the wheel round of the Mayan calendar are a few examples.

The earliest record that may have been found is of a Mesolithic woman, found by archaeologists buried with large stones placed in a circle. Though it is highly theoretical, some archaeologists refer to her as the first shaman. Even the stones and their placement are a source of controversy. There were some stones placed upon her body while others are situated around her. Some report that it was not a complete circle and represented something else, while others argue that the stones shifted through time, about 12,000 years. Some argue that the stones had a role as a gateway to other worlds. Regardless of what the truth may be, which will never truly be known, it is simply another example of the wheel of life appearing in very early times.

Circles of stones have been found on the ground in a variety of locations and have been thought to be aligned with the geographic features of the land and to astrological events. The planet is covered with circles within circles, from time immemorial to the present day. These circles are most often associated with spiritual practices of one kind or another, despite different eras, cultures, belief systems and symbology. Simply put, there is no one singular path, no one truth, to the circle of life.

SACRED CEREMONIES

Every teacher, every tradition, every lineage will have various medicine and various beginnings to ceremony with regards to the Medicine Wheel. It is the intent here to offer contemporary and simple ceremonial ways that all may follow as a basis to begin. Not everyone begins upon the wheel journey in the same place, but for our purposes, we will begin with the East. Still, keep in mind, as one teacher of mine shared – it matters less where you begin, than that you begin.

A sacred ceremony is an outward and physical representation of your intentions. The Medicine Wheel is an outward and physical creation of dialogue we have with Great Spirit within ourselves. Thus, a sacred ceremony allows us to begin the dialogue and is a mirror that we can look into, that will reflect back all that is within us and the world around us.

As each person has a different internal dialogue with Great Spirit, each wheel will be different, each walk will be different and each ceremony will be different. In addition, each of us has a different vision, a different purpose, and a different intent. What is important is to have a focused point for the dialogue. The Medicine Wheel is a focal point for that dialogue. Both dialogue and wheel will become deeper, woven with different threads of the great tapestry of life. Like any great tapestry, it will grow richer, deeper in color and more opulent in dimension. The wheel, in all its richness, is a model, a tool, to be used to learn the dance of life, to shift perception and to add clarity to a journey.

Tradition is something that is passed down from one to another. Each time a tradition is shared, it shape shifts. It changes based on our experience. It shifts depending on our intent. The basis of all tradition is sacred intent. Every ceremony is based upon someone's tradition. Think of a wedding – is a hand fasting any less sacred than a traditional Catholic mass? Not really. Different tools – different words – same intent. Either way, two people are entering a sacred contract. It is the same with a

Medicine Wheel ceremony – a sacred contract to walk the wheel is being made. It is YOUR contract – YOUR intent that is vital here. This is why we began with what is sacred to you. What do you value? What do you wish to gain from the journey? It is vital to know these things before beginning a ceremony. I can guarantee you the ceremony you enter into now will be different than the ceremony you enter into a year from now. Sacred intent, however, will be the same.

This is a simple brief overview of the directions to prepare for a beginning ceremony. We will be going beyond the four cardinal directions. Think of it this way: this is the entire wheel of life, not a single moment within it. We will dive into the river deeper in future chapters.

Direction	East	South	West	North
Time of Day	Sunrise	Noon	Sunset	Midnight
Seasons	Spring	Summer	Fall	Winter

East	Newness and beginnings
Southeast	Healing to the highest good
South	Nurturing and emotion
Southwest	Dreaming and visioning – spiritual action
West	Death and release
Northwest	Teaching and knowledge – truths
North	Knowledge and germination

| Northeast | Chaos and the Warrior that empowers |
| Center | Above and Below- Father Spirit and Mother Earth – God and Goddess |

CEREMONY TO HONOR THE WHEEL OF LIFE

We will begin with a simple ceremony that honors the entire Wheel of Life rather than a singular portion of the wheel. It is in honoring the entire wheel that we honor all that we are and that life is. We are all one.

This ceremony can be done anywhere. The center of the wheel, that hub where you stand at the moment within your soul, it is not a geographical location. You can draw a wheel on the floor and focus on it as you honor it. You can go outside in nature and look to the directions as you honor them. You can create small symbolic wheels that represent each of the aspects of the directions to you.

Begin any sacred ceremony with a cleansing. Whether you are using smudge, camphor, or intent by simply asking that you be cleansed of all that is not of benefit to your highest good – it is the act of preparing yourself for a sacred ceremony that is the essence of cleansing.

In honoring and invoking the directions, you may in your own way simply offer a prayer. You can stand in each of the directions and make an offering, for example, of cornmeal (birds love it!) or fresh flowers. You can begin in the direction that feels appropriate to you as long as you honor all the directions. Allow the circle to shape itself as you give it physical form, creating it with your movements and intentions.

You might want to put fire at the center, or hub, of the wheel. If you are indoors, you could use a candle, or outdoors a full fire or a torch light may be your representation for the center. To create the circle around that center, you could place a stone in each of the directions, for example, along with your offering. Make the wheel as simple or as decorative as you want – it is your wheel.

Prior to your prayer and lightning the central fire (if you choose to have a fire), you will want to do your intentional cleansing. Once the fire is ignited, offer your prayer of intent.

DIRECTIONS PRAYER

An honoring prayer to the directions that can be used in beginning a walk of the Medicine Wheel

Great Spirit, the Creator of All, we pray to open our hearts, open our souls that we may feel and breathe in the new waves of energy that now flow to us from the Divine Source of All Things.

We pray that as our Mother Earth awakens and a new global world begins to emerge that you grant us our own voices to speak our own truths.

The Great Spirits of Skies, we pray that healing happens within each of us to prepare for this new journey. A deep healing that releases and purifies the soul from limitations, lacks and old belief systems that no longer serve our higher good. We pray that each of us following this journey easily and effortlessly let go of pain and separation, that the eternal flames transform us, allowing us to become a beautiful Phoenix rising up from the ashes to be our authentic selves.

Almighty we pray that you bless us with courage to become fearlessly empowered with your inspiration and passion that we may soar through all spiritual challenges between the worlds as your divine warriors. We pray that you become our bridge of light to our divinity giving us the faith and strength to walk as empowered souls with truth, passion and eternal love.

Spirit of the skies above, we are filled with gratitude and overflowing love for all the blessings you have bestowed upon us, for all the moments you carried us when we could not walk ourselves, for the moments you radiated love gifting us overflowing joys, and for the moments you transformed our tears into laughter.

Spirits of the east, in humble reverence we come in gratitude for the morning light that you grace us with every day. We ask you bring your powers of illumination and awakening to spring forward the awareness that we may be reborn with the eyes of a newborn.

Spirits of the southeast, in humble reverence we come in gratitude for the healing given each day. We ask you bring your powers of healing to our souls, our hearts, and our bodies so that we may rise to our highest good.

Spirits of the south, in humble reverence we come in gratitude for the living in life every day. We ask you bring your powers of breath that we may know more fully our truth within self. Teach us and show us the good relationship with all things and the gifts you bestow.

Spirits of the southwest, in humble reverence we come in gratitude for the visions and dream you give to us. We ask you bring your powers of the journey that we may better understand your messages of action.

Spirits of the west, in humble reverence we come to you as the dusk of sunset arrives upon the horizon. We ask you bring your powers of unity forward as we mature in our awareness. Dissolve the boundaries that separate us from unity with one another. Share with us the responsibility of growing into maturity.

Spirits of the northwest, in humble reverence we come in gratitude for the truths you have revealed to us. We ask that you bring your powers to reveal the soul truths of your wisdom found within each of us.

Spirits of the north, in humble reverence we come in gratitude for the wisdom you have shared and for the dark cover that has germinated the seeds. We ask you to bring your powers to sharing clarity and purity of thought within the deep contemplation of stillness.

Spirits of the northeast, in humble reverence we come in gratitude for the warrior spirit that empowers us. We ask that you bring your powers to strengthen our spirits and grace us with the courage to face ourselves.

Spirits of Mother Earth, in humble reverence we come in gratitude for all you give to us each day in our food, in our air, in our water, in our fires. We ask that you share your powers of life. Teach us to give in abundance as you give to each of us in abundance. Thank you for cradling us and nurturing us each day.

Spirits of Father Sky, in humble reverence we come in gratitude for the light of days and the dark of nights. We ask that you share your powers of life to awaken the light of spirit within us all. We give gratitude for our breath.

We thank you Great Spirit for the beautiful canvas painted across our skies each sunrise and each sunset. We pray that each one reveals a deeper understanding and love for the web of life.

It is within this gratitude, and it is within this Eternal love, that we ask these things for our journey.

What is really important?

- Know your intent – why are you walking the spokes.
- Know what you hold sacred as belief.
- Know that this is a sacred act of power.

With that in mind, be sure to give thanks, ask for what you wish to receive, and say thank you again. Honor and celebrate your intentions.

Whenever you are create a container in which others will hold ceremonies, your words will be more universal. But this personal ceremony is about you, your act of power, and your journey.

Ceremonies teach us how we use our spiritual senses to see into the spirit world and to gain universal knowledge. At the same time these Medicine Wheel ceremonies teach us to move with the spirit. By using the Medicine Wheel and the four wind directions, we learn to build our own permanent wheel.

Sacred ceremonies teach us to depend upon our spiritual senses, to hear the whispers in the winds, and to move with spirit.

Sacred ceremony around the wheel can provide a structure for daily application of spiritual principles. It provides for inspiration in journaling, dream work, and meditation so that you can discover the answers to the questions you ask yourself such as, "Who am I? Where do I come from? Where am I going?" In any ceremony, it is vital to honor your own path, your own space, your own connection with spirit. The gift of sacred ceremony around the wheel is the insight and clarity you can receive in order to bring balance and harmony to your inner spirit.

The first ceremony described is the beginning of our first journey around the wheel. We learn in this first ceremony how to gain clarity and wisdom through the spokes. It is our first journey to breathe in the teachings.

The second ceremony or second walk of the Medicine Wheel is where we begin to experience the elements and meet the animals who travel with us on our journeys as our guides and protectors. We learn of our shadow here and the forms that it takes on.

The third ceremony or third walk of the Medicine Wheel is where we experience our own personal medicine. It is here that our awareness in our world is shown and how we may heal our whole being.

The fourth ceremony or fourth walk of the Medicine Wheel is where we return to our origin and our own ancestors to connect with our ancient knowledge. It is here that we begin to remember our origin, remember who we are and our purpose of being.

There are also special ceremonies that occur around the Medicine Wheel for various aspects of the cycle of life.

SACRED CEREMONY FOR WOMEN

Women follow the cycle of the moon. This ceremony honors woman for her nurturing and love of self and all that surrounds her. It celebrates the gift of life, the gift of her blood as life, and her feminine power. The sacred ceremony around the wheel honors the many aspects of a woman's life. The wisdom of the maiden, mother, and the crone all teach women to reclaim her own power and stand as a vital part of the circle, equal to the masculine. The warrior within the feminine is explored as well as the goddess each woman is.

SACRED CEREMONY FOR PERSONAL MEDICINE

A person with specific needs, specific intentions, or who seeks a deeper transformation in a particular area can perform a ceremony that is a spiritual inventory walk. It allows for continued growth and transformation in specific areas. It can be used to explore a shadow aspect of self to develop a specific archetype energy that is weaker in nature.

Personal medicine ceremonies can also be used as group medicine. Women gathering together may incorporate individual ceremonies into their group gathering ceremony. Business owners can use the same aspects to discover what is lacking within their business plans and strategies to incorporate a balanced and harmonious approach to their business.

SACRED CEREMONY REBIRTH FIRE

This is a sacred ceremony done in a renewal or rebirthing transformation process that allows you to discover the guidance of the journey ahead. Many times this is a ceremonial walk done through the vision quest.

SACRED CEREMONY FOR MEN

This is a sacred ceremony done for the masculine energies, and to balance the warrior spirit with the nurturing energy. This ceremony heals the duality of energy within the active energy. It teaches the silence that is vital to hear the answers much like the silence that the hunter has to track its prey. It teaches the wisdom of integrity, spiritual obligations, and the tenacity of authentic voice.

SACRED CEREMONY FOR COMMUNITY

This is a sacred ceremony that is done within a community or those who walk the path of a leader. It reveals the in-depth complexity of compromise, peace among all, and the balance between innocence and defending your truths. It shares the awareness of consequences of action.

This ceremonial walk is used often by councils to make decisions upon issues which affect the whole.

There are sacred ceremonial walks that can be done for nearly every aspect of life including any archetype energy that one may wish to explore.

These are only examples of the various sacred ceremonies that can use the Medicine Wheel teachings. The teachings are based on unity and represent that all of life is a cycle – or, simply put, all is one. The ceremonies and teachings offered in this book give a practical application to understanding the complexity of life and to answer the questions of the soul. They help balance duality so we can merge into oneness. They are tools for growth and transformation in life.

CHAPTER 7

THE CARDINAL DIRECTIONS

There are as many variations of the medicine wheel as there are places upon Mother Earth. All have one common thread within them; they look to nature for the medicine of the wheel. Nature reveals how energy is flowing. The nature of the energy, the direction of flow, and the representation of the energy through symbols, animals, and colors all will differ depending upon what one sees when they step into nature to listen.

Yet, they all represent the four directions and the center point. What the directions represent goes back to the geographical location. The variation does not mean that one teaching is truth nor does it mean it is false. It simply means that as one stands to look across the universe before them is coming from a different perspective. To find your own inner truth, you must find your own medicine. When we adopt the teachings of another we simply are accepting another's truth as our own. This will leave us wanting and yearning. It is to read another's experience and accepting it without having our own experience.

As you begin this journey notice what creatures from Mother Earth enter your path, what colors, and what dreams you have. Allow the mystery of the medicine to unfold for you. Allow yourself to experience. As one experiences for themselves the medicine, it is then that one can be in the knowing of their own wisdom.

The medicine wheel is a sacred tool which allows us to dive into our own wisdom within to find the answer of who we are authentically, what our Divine purpose is, and the map to get there. The cardinal directions are the basic representations of the wheel. In its physical form it is a circle with a cross in the middle. It is very much like a compass with each spoke a pathway for us to follow. When we create a physical representation it is a sacred form allowing us to experience in a deeper way the medicine of the direction.

THE EAST

The east is representative of the dawn of awakenings; the spring of life. It is those "aha" moments in life that allow a new awareness. The spring of life that births new visions. It is the illumination cycle where awareness brings into vision of birth to life. It is the hour of Dawn and ideas flowing freely into the circle of life. The East is the place that opens perceptions and the mind to new ideas.

It is the place where the day begins, with the sun rising high into the sky from the east, and it is the springtime. The Wheel uses the beginning of each day as the time when the sun rises for you. Your birth is the East in your own life time. The First day of the year is the full Moon of the equinox when the peak strength of the sun is above.

Why is the sun so important to each of us? Beyond the physical, it is the power of light that allows a person to see with clarity. It can also be said that the Power of light allows clear vision. The plants of the Earth strive to burst forth to reach the light of the sun. It is also the light that reveals the power of enlightenment.

Although we can watch the sun rise, the understanding and need for the power of light is not always visible to the physical eye. As with all things, the sun has both positive and negative energies within it. The power of enlightening can cause a person to become enlightened only to become cynical in perspective or it can cause one to become wise in knowledge.

It is said that in the sacred moment of dawn, when the sun births from the horizon to illuminate a new day, that all the creatures, the winds, the oceans pause to stand in silent witness to the birth. This teaching reminds us that just as the sun rises each morning to shine its light upon Mother Earth; so too does the Great Spirit emerge to shine a birthing light when we find ourselves lost in perpetual darkness if only we will pause in the sacred moment. The balance between the light and darkness is essential to life.

The recognized knowledge and energy within the universe is what the workings of the wheel are all about. When you begin to see, feel, and understand it then when you begin to give honor to all things. This is the connection of the medicine wheel.

Within the power of the light and the East, the Eagle is representative of it. The eagle can see with clear vision from great heights in the sky. The East is a place of clear vision that allows enlightenment which represents what color? The color of the East is a perceptive one. Since you are the center of your own medicine wheel the color one will see will be different. I see the color of opalescent white. The white light is brightest. It defines all other colors from it. It allows the prisms to gift us with colors of the rainbow. There is no right or wrong color to see. There is only your color.

The East is beginnings. This is the power of dependency; the power of a new babe emerging from the womb. Within the East everything must be provided from outside of you. The sun provides the power and the light, just as a new babe is given dependency upon the mother who births her. The East gave birth to the Sun first and then to you.

The East Wind is used to bring new beginnings and new projects.

THE SOUTH

The south is representative of the midday heat of life. The summer season in the cycle is where things need water and to be nurtured. The South is an active place of growth where hearts and souls are warmed; where trust and innocence spin with the confusion of life. It is the part of the circle where work must be done, active growing happens and where we reflect upon life to see the future crops.

When working with a medicine wheel, we move in a circle from East to South. This is the same movement that the sun makes. The South is the part of the day from when the sunrises to noon. It is springtime to summer. It is the growth from an infant to a child. This movement involves many different phases of the cycle within.

The power of the South embodies curiosity. We see that in a small child who endeavors to find out all things about all things.

The animal of the South is often the mouse. It is a small animal that comes in groups and is inquisitive and curious about all things. This also falls into innocence and trust. Just as a small child has the innocence to trust all things so does the mouse. The power of the south teaches us to trust the truth. Believe with the innocence of a small child or a small mouse. This is the power of the South.

The color of the south for me is bright red. Why? Noon time is the hottest part of the day. The sun is straight above shining the heat of its energy upon me. It causes my skin to redden. It is the color of spirit. Summertime with the innocence and trust entwined with curiosity creates a spiraling spirit of rapid activity.

The South Wind is most powerful time to build and expand. The Summer Solstice is the day with the longest light and therefore is the most powerful day of the South. Call upon the South wind for help in seeking ways of learning to expand your life.

THE WEST

The west is representative of the twilight of life. It is a time to look within and being grateful for the harvest that is being collected. The West is time to release, just as the leaves fall from the trees in the autumn. The sun begins to fade and go beyond the horizon at dusk and cleaning and cleansing time begins to prepare for winter. It is time for pruning those areas of life that have grown wild in order that new blooms may again emerge in the spring.

The West is the time of adulthood. In the year it is the fall, when things come to maturity. They have reached the phase of their development where physically they cannot grow anymore; just as an adult. Innocence and curiosity give way to wisdom and experience. It is the time in life when we begin to realize how little we really do know.

It is a time of fear and darkness. The sun sets in the west and the color of the west shifts from the bright red to a blue or deep purple into blackness; darkness. It is a time to look within, to discover our own fears and to reflect. The West is a time for self-discovery of who you really are. As fall begins, we discover what things we like, what things we do not like and understand that the power to change is within ourselves. It is time for our spirit or soul to emerge.

The power animal of the West is often the bear or the thunderbird. Nearly every Native American tribe known show the thunderbird in its art and imagery. When time was beginning and all things shared equally and all lived in complete harmony, there was one that had nothing to give but the beauty and the sound of its song. The simplicity of the thunder bird is its power.

Thunder beings are part of the fall. The dark skies begin to fill with thunder and lightning. The red hawk is now the thunderbird. It does the biddings of the rains and gives the gift of the blood of life.

This is where the rain dances came into being. The Thunderbirds simplistic song and their dance across the sky were thought to bring the blood of life - the rains are imitated through the rain dance. But through this power and gift, also comes fear and destruction. This is the true nature of the power of the West.

The West wind can help bring balance and equality. The stone for the West Wind is obsidian. It is an imperfect stone like no other with the light within the dark. When you want the fruits of your labors, the west wind will bring them.

THE NORTH

The north is representative of a time of rest. It is a time to germinate seeds for spring after the cleansing of fall. It is where the distilling of life happens during the cold winter months. It is a symbolic death, a dormant time, to allow release and renewal that only occurs when stillness happens. The North is the place to find wisdom and clarity of mind.

In the cycle of the year, the North is wintertime; the time of cold and of rest. Just as the plants, we within our own wheel need to take time for rest. It is the time from sunset to sunrise.

The white giant of the North lays its blanket over Mother Earth so that she too may rest. The darkness of the North makes exact timing difficult to have clarity of vision. It is easy to say that there is old age; however, when does that begin?

The power of the North is wisdom. It is the time when one can look back and reflect upon the enlightenment and self-discovery parts of life and simply know. Wisdom and knowledge are very different terms. One can have knowledge and have no wisdom at all. Wisdom gives clear insight within. It is finding that all knowledge can be of benefit.

It is a time to rest and reflect, to remember and keep before sharing the stories. It is a time to no longer seek guidance but to give it. It is a time to reflect on the consequences of knowledge and share with others about those consequences. It is not the ending but the beginning. It is said that wisdom is the most elusive of all powers that one can obtain. It slips from our grasp if we strive to hard for it. Yet it comes not at all when not sought. It is a time for knowing how much to give and how much to keep. The cycle comes to its natural conclusion.

The North Wind is a time to hold and keep reflecting on. The Winter Solstice is a day when the wisdom of the elders can help bring greater understanding into your life. The energy is rejuvenating itself.

The lessons within the Medicine Wheel are numerous. The wisdom and strength it can provide a person will carry you through the cycles of your life whether they are the cycles of your day, your life or your year.

Journal exercise:

In your journal take time to write what each of the cardinal directions represent to you. What is the wisdom you resonated most within the winds?

CHAPTER 8

FOUR BODIES EQUAL ONE WHOLE

Each direction represents stages of life. When we think of the life cycle of a butterfly as an example, we see it is not only the human life that is represented but all life.

N
Egg

Butterfly   Larva (Caterpillar)
  W   E

Pupa (Chrysalis)
S

STAGES OF LIFE

The North begins with the egg. As the egg germinates, a caterpillar is birthed. The caterpillar turns into the chrysalis, which then metaphorically becomes a butterfly. The butterfly lays an egg and the process begins again. It is much the same with the human life cycle.

N

<pre>
                    Death

   Maturity   Birth
       W   E

                    Growth
                       S
</pre>

LIFE CYCLE

The East is the birth phase of life. The infancy stage is where one is born into a "tribe" of biological family.

The South is the growth phase of life. The adolescent stage is where one begins to become an individual.

The West is the maturity phase of life. The maturity stage is where we see without blame or judgment discovering our own integrity.

The North is the elder into death phase of life. The death phase of life is where one has mindful detachment able to teach the wisdom has gained.

There is also a balance found in the wheel.

FOUR BODIES EQUAL ONE WHOLE

The four bodies are interconnected and interrelated. Let's say a person has a healthy physical body, lives a healthy lifestyle with diet and exercise. Perhaps they even pray and meditate daily, they can still find that they are out of balance and create dis-ease. If this same person is holding a deep resentment in their emotional body, it can cause the mental body to harbor stress. When a person is stressed they release stress hormones into the physical body. The resentment makes a connection to the spiritual body as the person will have a difficult time connecting to anything outside of themselves. The longer the resentment is held, the more dis-ease is created. Eventually the stress hormones will weaken the immune system, the continued resentment turns the thought energy to be fueled by negative energy and the deeper it becomes, the deeper the rift becomes in making that spiritual connection. It becomes a vicious cycle that creates the belief patterns that prevent a person from having a well-balanced life in all areas.

The four bodies energetically create an interwoven web that connects a person's perceptions, beliefs, and emotions. This interwoven web affects every aspect of life and has the ability to manifest the reality either a positive fulfilled life or a life of imbalance, stress, and hopelessness. The key to the math of four equals one is to have each of the energetic bodies in balance so that four equal parts become one whole being.

In the east we find the representation of the spiritual body. Regardless of what your belief system is, the spiritual body exists. It is where your personality exists. Your characteristics. It is where the soul or your light body exists.

The spiritual body is within a person from birth.

In the south we see the emotional body. Your emotions have a direct effect on your physical and mental bodies. Consider for a moment the emotion of anger. When a person becomes angry they scream, release adrenaline, and the nervous system goes into the "flight or fight" mode.

Every emotion, whether it is a positive emotion or a negative emotion, has an effect on the physical and mental bodies. When negative emotions continue for an extended period they create "toxins" on the energetic level. These "toxins" cause the immune system to become depressed, chronic fatigue, and can manifest into actual physical "dis-ease".

The longer a person holds onto the negative emotions the deeper ingrained within the mental body the "toxins" become. This constant barrage results in harmful belief patters to be created. It can even lead to our emotional body believing that in order to protect itself that it needs to stop experiencing any feelings at all. The results are not even being able to experience positive emotions.

In the west we see the physical body.

The physical body is what you see in the morning and the internal mechanisms that sustain physical life. The body is an amazing mechanism when you think about it. It knows automatically from birth how to do literally thousands of tasks from breathing and digesting to carrying life supporting blood, it even has a system that "protects" the body on certain levels through the immune system. Yet, this amazing mechanism is a fragile and vulnerable until that can become "broken" or imbalanced in an instant.

Although all that can be seen in the reflection is the outer shelf, there exist and energetic body that has its own vibrational rate. If any part of the physical body becomes clogged or blocked, it negatively affects the other three bodies of the whole. Toxins from the foods ingested, bacteria from the environment, and even the air that is breathed can create a blockage. Your diet, sleep habits, and the amount of exercise all have either a positive or negative effect on the physical body.

In the north, we find the mental body. Thoughts and intellect store the experiences a person has throughout their life. Thoughts are another form of energy. This thought form energy is what causes the electrical energetic pulses in your brain that create "wires" to stimulate the mind. The energy of your every thought is literally transformed into your beliefs.

Once the energetic thought is created it causes an imprint of that thought in your mental body very much like a blue print. This blue print is stored in the subconscious mind. The subconscious mind does not have the ability to rationalize whether the thought form is positive or negative. It simply accepts all thought forms and imprints them. Science has shown that the average person has approximately one hundred thousand thoughts every minute of every day. The implications of even half those thought form being negative is powerful.

When all four bodies are balanced a person will feel centered, focused and full of life. Ignoring one aspect affects the whole.

N
Mental

Physical   Spiritual
W   E

Emotional
S

Four Bodies

So as we explore the four bodies we look towards the east which is our spiritual side. It connects us with the world that we live in. Moving to the southeast with learn to live in balance with self between the spiritual and the emotional aspects of our being. The south is our emotional being, our heart. It is a reflection of our feelings. The southwest teaches us to live in balance with others as we experience the reflection of our emotions. The west is our physical body. Our engagement and action of life, how we take the emotions and spiritual connections and live them. The northwest teaches us how to live in balance with the land as we engage our physical actions. As we move to the north of our mental mind we generate understanding in life. The northeast teaches us to live in balance with creation. From all our experience and understanding we return to the spiritual.

Journal Exercise:
Think about your life on the medicine wheel, not your physical age, but your spiritual life. Where are you? Remember it is all about cycles, so one could be re-emerging into the spring cycle or one could be in the maturity of life.

THE MEDICINE WHEEL AS A COMPASS

Every compass has four different directions that are simultaneous in nature that offer different perceptions of the same question. Even when a question is placed in a direction, each will see it differently based upon their experience with the direction. The reason? The direction is power. The wheel itself, each direction upon the wheel is a mirror which everything within you is reflected back.

The Medicine Wheel is a dynamic and animate living being that has depth as expansive as the journey of life itself. The idea of using the wheel as a compass will allow a person to use the wheel and its medicine as an asset map to identify both the strengths and the shadows within a person.

By answering simple questions we can see what our internal strengths are in living:

What are your gifts of the mind? Of the heart? Of the body? Of the Spirit? What is your passion?

By answering the simple questions, we begin to map out our assets.

To create the compass in its simplest form, we begin with a ceremony.

As we stand in the center of our own world, it can be confusing which direction we are supposed to go. We can become confused about what our purpose is, where we are going and even how we are supposed to find our way to get there. The Medicine Wheel is a way to have communion between the Sacred and your own inner spirit.   For me, I look to the Medicine Wheel for my direction. The Medicine Wheel shows me the flow of my own energy as it correlates to the energy of the universe around me.

The Medicine Wheel that I share shows the four directions, the four wind directions and the center where I am. It shows both the external wheel and the internal wheel. The external wheel is representative of the universe and the internal wheel representative of the life that is created and exists within myself. Each of the eight directions is represented by a different element that exists in nature.

There are many ways to create the natural elements to use. In different paths that I have studied, the elements are different. No specific way is "The Way" or correct. Each person stands in a different center and sees things in different ways. Each of the directions provide opportunity to nurture and honor the both the directions and your own inner Spirit.

Your journey on the Medicine Wheel is really a personal story about your journey right now. It is seeing that your life is as sacred as the Earth you walk upon. It is really about opening your eyes and awakening into your own personal truths.

To begin in a simple way, let us use the Four Sacred Directions alone.

Begin by finding a special place to you. A place that you feel comfortable and enjoy being in. It can be in the middle of the living room or outside in nature. It really does not matter. On this simple Medicine Wheel we will use North as grounding, East as change, South as passion, and West as power and the center as spirit. This may change for you as you begin to spend more and more time with the Medicine Wheel.

Gather anything that is sacred to you in your life; a carving, a stone, a picture, or a piece of jewelry. When you have gathered 5 items for your wheel, sit down on the ground or floor to begin.

Pause for a moment and take a deep breath inward and exhale slowly to calm your insides and say a prayer in your tradition. Ask that it shows you to change the direction of your life. As that it shows you where you need to heal. Ask that the sacred space that is the Medicine Wheel protect you and comfort you. Let your own spiritual journey guide your prayers.

Remember, it does not matter what you place in each direction. There is no right or wrong here. This is your Medicine Wheel for your direction.

Place your hand down where the East of your wheel is. Think about change. Think about how the wind and air change the landscape of the Earth. Select one of the five items to place in the East that represents change. If you are having a difficult time choosing, simply close your eyes and select an item.

Move your hand to the South and place your hand on the ground here. Think about passion. Think about energy and fire and how the passion of love changes things. Again, select an item to represent the South.

Move your hand to the West and place your hand on the ground here. Think about power. Think about the power of healing. Think about water and how water changes the landscape. Think about your own dreams. Again, select an item to represent the West.

Move your hand to the North and place your hand on the ground here. Think about grounding. Think about your family. Think about the Earth itself. Think about what makes you personally feel safe on Earth. Again, select an item to represent the North.

Now put your hand in the center of the circle. This center is your spirit, your life. Think about your spiritual center, about who helps you and guides you in your spiritual journey. Think about those here on Earth and those from other worlds and the heavens that help and guide you. Place the last item in the center.

As you look at the Medicine Wheel in front of your, you begin to realize what areas of your life that are the strongest and what areas are the weakest. If you are not seeing a direction in which to begin, say another prayer. Close your eyes and ask that the wheel be blessed. Ask that it change your life and give you direction. Thank the Wheel for its inspiration and guidance.

You have created your first Medicine Wheel in its simplest form. You may not have gotten the neon sign you were hoping for, but you must, realize that you have only taken a baby step on the journey. If you can come to quiet yourself enough, the winds will speak to you and share their message. The Winds are what lies in between the directions. The Divine of your path speaks in these winds.

The Medicine Wheel is about creating, transforming, healing, learning, and guiding you on a journey. The more you step into it and work with the power of the Wheel, the more you will feel the sacred journey.

CHAPTER 9

CREATING THE WHEEL SPOKES

The Cardinal Directions share the quadrants most often used in Medicine Wheels. The spokes are a reflection of the personal medicine I have found in working with the Sacred Circle of Life. The directions were shared with me in the sweat lodges. As I was taught, in order to facilitate a sweat lodge, one must journey in a lodge with the doors facing in each direction (N, NE, E, SE, S, SW, W, NW, and W). Within each of these lodges there are eight seats using the same directions that one must journey in. So, as an example, one must enter an East lodge (Spring) eight times to sit in each of the seats within before moving into the South East lodge to continue on. This is 64 lodges and 64 journeys. Then one must be the fire keeper for a lodge in each direction before one can facilitate their own sweat lodges. That is the practical application of where the medicine wheel teaching originated for me.

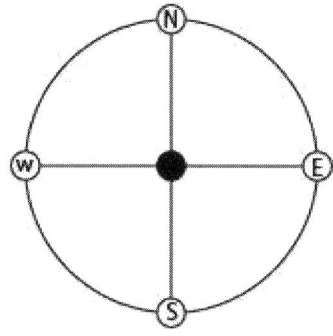

Center Hub

Imagine a center stone, a single stone; this is the center.

The Center Hub – The Center of all things - The Great Mystery. The Void. It is the center of all things. In a personal Medicine Wheel, as we are working with it – it is your center.

Now place a stone in the North, East, South and West. Draw imaginary lines to the center stone and from N-E-S-W. This is your center hub spokes. Here lies the power of life.

Spirit Keeper of the East - In the east is the web of life and represents new birth; infancy.

Spirit Keeper of the South - In the south is the human family and represents the growth of adolescence.

Spirit Keeper of the West - In the west is unity and the experience that comes with maturity.

Spirit Keeper of the North - In the north is the Great Family and represents the wisdom of old age.

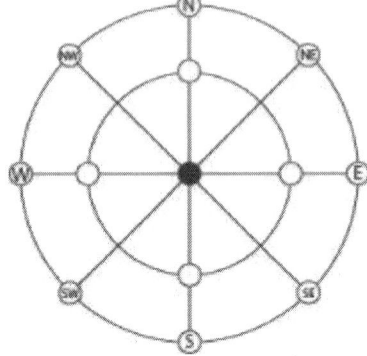

Inner Spokes

Now place stones a few inches above the north stone, then in the northeast, east, southeast, south, southwest, west, northwest, north and the north east. Draw imaginary lines between the N-NE-E-SE-S-SW-W-NW. Draw imaginary lines between the N and inner spokes N, NE and inner spokes of N and S, and so forth. This creates your Inner spokes and represents oneness with self in the personal medicine wheel.

- East – Tribe – Foundation
- Southeast – Relationships with ancestors to present

88

- South – Personal power
- Southwest – Divine Power
- West – Will power
- Northwest – Power of reasoning
- North – Gateway to the Divine
- Northeast – Power of the Warrior Spirit

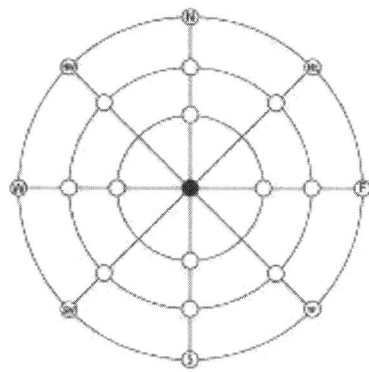

Outer Spokes

Now repeat placement of the stones for the outer spokes outside each of the inner spoke stones, drawing the same imaginary lines. These outer spokes of the personal Medicine Wheel represent unity – all are related and how we relate to each facet of life.

- East – Relatedness of Mother Earth
- Southeast - Relatedness of 2 legged
- South - Relatedness of swimmers
- Southwest - Relatedness of plants

- West - Relatedness of bugs, snakes and lizard world
- Northwest - Relatedness of 4 legged
- North - Relatedness of winged
- Northeast - Relatedness of the Universe

There are various thoughts on where to begin. Even with my own teachers, they had different methods that they worked with. One belief is that the wheel is also a spiral and it should begin in the outer spoke and work as a spiral inward to the center. Others believe that the spiral does not end and you work from the center outward.

Tradition begins with a single person repeating the same action year after year. This is my tradition of walking the spokes of the Medicine Wheel. The first week is spent in reflection of gratitude; gratitude for the gifts and blessings that I have received over the past year. Gratitude for the people in my life that are new friends and old ones, those I have watched cross over into the Summerlands and those who are here on the physical plane. My gratitude tree is overflowing with hearts that contain the names of those who have touched my life in some way over the years.

The second week is walking the outer spokes of the wheel, reflecting upon the interrelated connection that one has with all things. The interrelated connection with nature, with the sun, with the moon, with the four legged friends, and with all things outside of self is examined, not only as a reflection of the relationship, but also an inventory of what imprints and energy signatures are in relationship to each of the spokes.

The third week is walking the inner spokes of the wheel. The inner spokes is a process of delving into the intimate relationship with self and with the Divine connection within. What has shifted? What expansion and awakening has occurred? What character and archetypes have entered and what has gone back into the shadows? What parts of self are on the other side of the energetic spectrum?

The fourth weeks is walking the center hub or the four cardinal directions into the center void. The center hub is a process of reflecting upon all that has been contemplated upon from the outer and inner spokes, the interconnected and interwoven threads, and ending with a vision quest to reach the void, the mystery within.

Every responsible business does an inventory to clear out the unsalable goods to make room for new and exciting products. This process is the inventory to clear out the inner self, discard beliefs and behaviors that no longer are valid, and make room for new expansion in spiritual growth.

The vital key of this process is honesty. The process is for you alone, not for anyone else. If you cannot be honest with yourself when answering the questions, you will only block yourself from the growth and expansion of your own journey. If you struggle with answering questions, ask your Divine Source for help. Ask your Divine Source to guide you in honest thought. The results of doing this honestly will astound you. A new perspective will emerge if you allow it.

I am going to share a traditional prayer with you using some of the language from a "cousin" as I was taught and remember that is a prayer of thanks

Kwey Michomis, Kwey Kokomis,
Kwey Kichi Manido
Megwetch for this day
Megwetch for my life,
Megwetch for the joy you bring me each and every day in the many ways that you do.

If you have collected your stones, having the layout of how they will be walked on this journey, your homework is to create your medicine wheel. It is important to remember that the wheel lives and breathes within you and the physical representation of the wheel is much like an altar space that is a sacred manifestation of your spirit. I have created a wheel as a full altar before with guardian stones, feathers, and the four sacred medicines upon it. I have created an outdoor altar where I have mounded dirt to use as a table and placed the wheel atop it. Yet, when I was bed ridden and ill, I had a large piece of paper that I drew the wheel upon and doodled representations of each stone as I "walked" the wheel. This journey (yes whenever I teach the wheel I too journey its spokes with you) I have decided to etch each stone collected by hand the symbol I was gifted as I contemplate the medicine of the spoke.

PRAYER

Oh, Great Spirit
Whose whispers I hear in the winds,
To inhale the morning air giving life to All
I pray my simple words are heard.
Allow my footsteps be light and full of beauty
My eyes see the miracle of flight.
Allow my ears to hear the songs of your winds,
My hands open to receive all that you gift.
Allow my soul to experience the eternal love
That my heart shares it with all I meet.

Oh, Great Spirit
Whose whispers I hear in the winds,
Gift my spirit your strength
That I may be strong in faith.
Gift my spirit your wisdom
That I may be clear in vision.
Gift my spirit your grace
That I may be compassionate to all.
As the sun rises across the skies
May I experience the joy of your creations.

CHAPTER 10

THREE WORLDS

THREE WORLDS

There are three "worlds" so to speak; the Lower world, the Middle world, and the Upper world. While they are really all the same "world", one can think of them as different dimensions that exist. So when we speak of journey's it is really multi-dimensional travel. Just as your body has a physical appearance, it also has a multi-dimensional appearance - a spiritual appearance.

MIDDLE WORLD

This is the reality that you live in in the physical. It is here on Earth. It is where you physical walk, talk, listen, taste, touch on a daily basis. It is the world that most of us are familiar with.

UPPER WORLD

This is the heavens. It is another dimension. It is the stars and the skies. It is other Universes. It also seems to be where most people 'think' they are going when they do any type of journey work.

LOWER WORLD

This is where most soul work happens. It is the place where your Akashi records are stored which may be why so many believe they are in the Upper worlds. The word akasha is Sanskrit and literally translates to mean "sky" or "ether". This is where your soul exists, where fragments that may have been lost are, and where your soul contracts can be renegotiated. This is where we will work.

While there are different experiences in each of these worlds, what I share (and really all I can share) is my experience. Journeys are something that anyone can practice and become adept in. They have been referred to as walking between the worlds, astral projection, remote viewing, and vision quests. In some ways each of these are different and in other ways they are very much the same.

Let's talk about the idea of time. Time is an illusion in the Middle world. We live in a linear time based society in the Middle world. The linear time frame goes like this - past, present, and future. The future never comes before the past. Yet, we talk about life being in cycles, in a circular motion. If that is true, which I believe it is, then the future always proceeds the past. In the Upper and Lower worlds time as we know it in the linear experience does not exist. Thus, when we journey we can go into the past or the future with ease. This is called interdimensional travel, past life regression or no time - depending on your theory of experience. These experiences can be brought back to the Middle world. The important aspect about time is to remember that time does not exist as we know it in the other worlds.

What does the other worlds look like? Well again this will depend upon your experience. There are some commonalities however. Every entrance to every part of all the Upper and Lower worlds will have a gatekeeper or a guide. Whether a person utilizes them or not is a choice. The gatekeeper really is who ensures that you will be protected, guided, and that your intentions are pure. They make the choice as to whether you are allowed to experience a journey or not. They can appear as a guide, a power animal, a warrior, a small child or as an image of self. The appearance will depend upon what you can resonate with at any given time. They will shape shift.

THE LOWER WORLD.

In this book we will be doing journey work on each of the spokes. We will enter the Lower World through l the Inner Temple. For each person this Inner Temple will appear to what resonates for them based upon their own experiences. My experience is that the Inner Temple is much like a cavern. It has a gate keeper that stands at its entrance, the center is a fire altar, and it is circular in shape. There are multiple archways - gateways - off the main temple. Each one is like a mine shaft. Each one leads to another chamber. So for example, there is a chamber referred to as the Origin chamber. From this chamber we can travel to the many past lives all the way back to the origin of the soul. There are shafts that one could follow to generational time threads - for example your father's family. It could take many, many lifetimes to even begin to explore all the shafts. This is where the soul fragments and pieces that I are within exist safe and protected. This is where soul retrievals are done.

There is also a chamber off the main Inner Temple referred to as the Knowledge chamber. This chamber has a book in the center on the altar. This is the book of records. It contains the stories of a person's life. This is how many people do past life regressions or read the Akashi records.

There is a chamber referred to as the Treasure Chamber. This is where a person can go to meet power animals, pick up tools for the spirit world and receive gifts from guides.

There is a Cauldron of the Soul chamber. This is where the spark of life for all souls exists; where our true authentic power lies. Our life force. There are many other chambers but this gives you an idea of the representation of my personal experience is. I have had others who do this work share that the Lower World for them is like going to visit a lush green patch of grass beneath the Tree of Life roots. A small brook flows near the grass and when they wish to go deeper; they ride a leaf down the river and exit where they are called to do so. There is no absolute truth here.

You will experience what will be clarity to you when you journey. It is vital to remember not to judge your experience. The biggest question asked is how does one know if it is imagination or a true journey? Here is a simple answer. If you can change it easily - it is imagination. Let me explain with an example. If you are wearing a blue shirt, and you can easily change it to a green dress - it is imagination not a journey. There are no absolutes in translating spiritual vibrations. Your guides and gatekeepers will share with you in a form that you can resonate with.

GROUNDING

Grounding is simply a way to connect yourself energetically to the core of the Earth energy. This will help you with inner focus for your intent. As there are many ways to ground yourself, simply try techniques until you find one that works for you.

The basic essence for most is to relax and visualize yourself connected to Earth. Some traditions visualize sending an energy cord or a light beam into the Earth from your root chakra (this is located in your tail bone) and send it directly into the center of the Earth.

The purpose of this is to tap into the core of the Earth's energy allowing you to receive energy through this cord or beam of light. Visualize it as a flush, as your energy goes down it is returned pure and whole. Once you feel the light beaming up to your root chakra feel it fill your entire being and reach the crown chakra (located at the top of your head) and beam upward connecting you to the Divine or the Universal Energy Force of the Cosmos.

Allow the pure light beam or cord to connect you from both the root chakra to the crown chakra; from the Earth to the Divine.

There is another classic form of grounding which is to image your feet as roots growing into the Earth. And allowing the Earth energy to flow up your spinal column (also called your central energy channel).

The visualization I most often use, when I use one, starts with dropping a cord of fire light from the heart, and or solar plexus, straight down the spinal channel to the center of the Earth. Or calling up a cord from the Earth center, which some people find easier, and then flowing it up to the spiritual center (sometimes going through the Sun). I then expand it to be a tube, encompassing my entire basic aura.

Eating, stomping your feet placing your hands on your thighs and intending to ground are some other methods there are dozens of different techniques and meditations for grounding and centering because these practices are a vital part of our personal wellbeing.

After spending a day journeying, to be honest the greatest tool for grounding is cleaning my toilets. There is no better way to truly get grounded back in the physical reality than cleaning a toilet bowl. It may sound funny, but try it sometime.

CONNECT TO SOURCE

You can also run a cord up or make an energy connection into the spiritual heart of the universe from your crown chakra while intending that you be aligned with the highest soul purpose while staying well connected to the physical plane.

That is you are contained within yourself and connected to Earth and the physical and to spiritual source at the same time in a harmonious balance with the universe

I always ground, center and clear before I begin a healing session or attunement in addition to connecting to the cosmic center and to activating the energies I am working with. I ground from my root chakra rather than from the legs because I got bad cramps in the legs when I grounded from the feet. I send a cord to the earth core asking earth for permission I widen the cord into a tube as wide as my aura and send negative energies down to be transformed to usable energy for the

Earth as well as calling up energies from Earth I send up to galactic universal center.

Some people feel best when they call the Earth energy up and call the cosmic energy down rather than sending up and down.

GROUNDING MEDITATION

You can do this meditation anywhere, however, I will tell you that I try to do this at least a few times a week barefoot outside burying my feet a few inches deep into the ground.

Begin by sitting comfortably with your spine in an upright position. Be sure your feet are flat on the ground. Take a deep breath in, inhaling through the nose filling your lungs fully and hold for a moment. Then exhale through your mouth. Now let's do that again. Inhale deeply through your nose and slowly exhale

See your feet down into the Earth rooting like the roots of a tree.

As you visualize the roots in the grounds anchoring you there for the moment, see them as hollow tubes that are that are going deep into the Earth. Connecting with her, feel the connection with the Earth and all of the gifts that she gives each day to us. Now I want to mentally ask with intention to draw up the pure energy of the earth up to these hollow tubes that are your roots in your feet

As you ask Mother earth intentionally, begin to see the molten lava that is within the center of the Earth and move up through these two tubes, these roots coming together into the hollowness of the trunk creating a cord.

Strengthening your connection feel the energy slowly come up through your legs as the hot lava simply warms you.

Feeling as though you're being in wrapped in a warm blanket. Feel the pulling at your hips allowing it to circulate drawing up now through your spine and to the top of your head feel the warming of every cell of your being as it spills over your head and back down to the ground going back down into the center of the Earth from where it came, creating a circuits of flowing energy flowing fire from the center of the earth up through your body flowing cleansing and grounding your primordial energy reservoir.

Allow it to bathe you fully in this restorative energy that comes from the center of the Earth anchoring you for the moment with this orange light. This orange energy of fire flowing from the tips of the toes as they are rooted deep into the Earth. Flowing up your legs and into your hips creating a spiral of energy as it flows up your spine through your stomach area. Up through your heart through your neck up into your head and spilling back out over you; creating a midline down through your center as it goes back into the earth from where it came in the cauldron of the Earth. Completing the circuit as it strengthens and grounds your nervous system knowing that as you feel this connection this grounding with Mother Earth you can recall this cord at any time that you need to get reconnected to get grounded.

Notice how it fills even the tips of your fingers as it flows outward allow the circuit to strengthen for a few more moments and know that each time that you repeat this grounding with Mother Earth your nervous system will calm that the toxins that you have collected throughout the day will be purified and returned to the Earth to be transmuted into usable energy.

Once this circuit has been established and you feel the energy flowing through you envision a large rose in front of you with a long thick stem that goes down through the Earth connecting in to your circuit. Set your intention that this beautiful rose in front of you is your heart chakra. It is where all of your emotions are in all their pure beauty and pure love. By your intention set this rose as a vacuum that is connected to your heart. Each time you encounter any negative energy negative emotions that the rose will act like a vacuum and suck the negative energy from you or that is directed toward you and shoot it down the cord to be mulched and composted by Mother Earth. It is always with you now that you're connected with Mother Earth and her circuits. Smell the sweet aroma that comes from her and know that each time you feel a negative emotions all you must simply do is inhale and remember the smell of the rose to have that energy transmuted and composted into usable energy by Mother Earth

Inhale deeply again in through the nose and up through the mouth feeling this connection and as soon as you are ready knowing that anytime you can return simply by inhaling and smelling the rose to the circuit and ground and purify your energy. When you're ready open your eyes and feel renewed.

BREATHING

Breathing! Simple breathing. It is something that we take for granted, yet, the act of breathing is a powerful tool whether you are using reverse breathing or embryonic breathing. The art of breathing is something that can raise your chi (your energy or life force), relax into self-hypnotic trance, or allow the "monkey mind" to come to stand still.

One style that increases energy and gathers your chi/life force. While there are a multitude of breath work that will do this is the form I most often use (for a variety of reasons). This is a powerful style of breathing that also returns you to your pre-birth state (which has its own benefits).

Embryonic breathing raises your chi in the deepest core of your center (Tan Tien) where it is stored in your energetic body for later use. The more chi you have, the more you can accomplish without a great deal of effort. My master can actually push someone over with one finger - again it is not due to the fact his finger is so strong, but due to the fact that his chi is that strong.

While in the womb, you breath all breath through the umbilical cord that is attached to the abdomen. As born humans, that is exactly the opposite of how we breathe. When we breathe we expand our abdomen in and deflate it when we exhale. It is believed that if we practice embryonic breathing we can regain our original tranquility and reclaim all the energy we incarnated with.

To practice - as you inhale let your abdomen gently contract as the chest expands. In a continuous flow, gently exhale allowing the chest to flatten while the abdomen expand. Breath very lightly and push very gently. Though you are gathering a powerful energy, this is very gentle in nature. Keep your attention and complete awareness on the air flow as it flows in and out. You want this to be a completely seamless continuous flow of breath with no pauses in between the inhale and exhale.

As you practice this, allow the length of the breaths extend. The area behind your belly, just between the belly button and public bone, will get warm (even hot) as you raise your chi. This is powerful work so only practice for short periods at a time. It can make you light headed as well so use caution when first practicing.

LITTLE DEATH

When you hear some speak of a journey you hear of things like drumming and rattles and crystal bowls and singing bowls all the way to things slate of psychedelic drugs. It was taught to me that if I cannot the journey by my own heartbeat but only with something external that I really had no business doing any type of journey into the Lower and Upper worlds.

The breathing exercise can bring you into the trance state of mind for journey work. It is called little death. You begin by touching the tip of your tongue to the roof of your mouth just behind your front teeth. Inhale deeply through your nose for a count of seven. Hold your breath in that state for a count of seven and then exhale through the mouth slowly for a count of seven. Then sit with no breath for a count of seven. So ideally the single breath will take approximately thirty seconds.

You work with that same pattern until you can reach completing the cycle seven times. You will feel light headed. Things will shift slightly as your subconscious fights for more breath. Take it slow as you practice don't try to do all once you know practice

As you practice this you want to make sure you comfortable and pressure of your feet are flat on the ground. You may experience the sound of breath or the sound of the heartbeat as you practice. This is normal. Just focus upon counting to begin and then you can switch to using your heartbeat as a drum beat.

SAFETY

Can you get lost?

Do you need an anchor?

Can you journey alone?

Safety, protection, does not exist - it is an illusion.

Why doesn't it exist? In order to receive you must allow. This means that in order for someone to "throw a hex" you must allow the energy of that "hex" in. If you don't allow it in - it can't affect you. Is it protection? Suppose depending upon your definition. What causes the deflection - your intention? You set the intention that you will only allow what is for your highest good. With that intention you are saying to the Great Spirit - whatever you deem in my highest good - not what I deem in my highest good. Now are there those both in the Middle world and other worlds that set out to screw with you - cause harm? Absolutely.

Are there people who use energy, manipulate it, and are malicious? Absolutely. Back to the seduction, if you know where you can be seduced, if you know where your fears are, if you know where your weaknesses are - then you can avoid most of what we call darkness in the Middle world.

Can you get lost? Absolutely.

Can you lose part of yourself on a journey? Absolutely.

Can you come back different? Absolutely.

We work diligently with grounding first- why? To set an anchor before we dived in. The anchor allows us to have an energetic thread to follow.

Gatekeepers. Your gatekeeper (guide), if asked, will guide you, offer a protective eye, and at times won't let you pass if they do not feel you are ready to go on. I have had many people tell me, this whole journey thing is not working for me. I listen. Many times they have not done the necessary work before hand, so the gatekeeper will not allow them to proceed. We worked on setting intention, creating sacred space, and grounding - each of these are building blocks. As you progress in your journey they will shapeshift and take on a deeper meaning that will be for you alone.

By visiting the Inner Temple, by meeting our guides/gatekeepers, by setting intentions we are preparing for deeper journeys. By learning about the chambers of the Lower world we are beginning to map our route. As we map our route, we are beginning the process of reclaiming our power. It is work. It is not a quick process. It takes practice. You get dirty. You get frustrated. You go through the full range of emotional experiences. But in the end, you know how to go find your true authentic self as a whole being

While reading the descriptions, it is like gazing at a postcard from Florida and seeing our beautiful beaches during the middle of a frozen north winter, it is vital to remember that the postcard won't put you on the warm sand, it won't warm up your toes, nor will it give you the experience of a sunburn. It is like the map to the destination - if our destination is the Lower World to discover our true authentic whole self - unless we put the dynamic action in of actually practicing each of the steps (grounding, intentions, breath work, etc.) we will not go on the journey.

Any time you are going to do journey work be sure to go through the process, ground yourself, create sacred space, set the intention and begin with your breathing. Ask for assistance, listen and remain observant and when you are done be sure to thank your gatekeeper, close your space and reground yourself.

There are times when Spirit or your gatekeeper (guides) will speak in a manner that is loud and crystal clear. When this happens, pause and ask again. Why? There are times when we all question what is being shared, the messages. It is sometimes the pause that makes sense of the messages. There is a difference between pausing and not doing. A pause is short - a pause one always spends time reflecting and contemplating.

There are times when our lives become very difficult on the physical journey. The drama of our stories are so really that it consumes us. The circumstances of our story become out of all control of our being. So how does one rise above? How does one let go of the drama? Let go of the story?

Have you ever looked at someone and said "well if I had their abilities" or "if I was strong like them"? Ever wonder where a person dives into and emerge from the waters with gifts that just astound the world around them? Whether it is strength, courage or something like painting, writing - the gifts are just amazing. These extraordinary gifts are not given just a select few - they are for each and every one of us. Everyone has the ability to receive, discover, and enjoy gifts. Here is the difference. Many are completely unaware that the special gifts are awaiting them, they settle into the drama - except that this is their plot in life and that they have not learned some lesson yet.

Some will call these gifts tools or attributes, but I will share that my experience is that they are medicine. They are deep and powerful medicine that when we pick them up and use them can allow a person to transform a circumstance and begin to manifest a new reality. One needs to remember that in the Lower World, these gifts, this medicine, can come to use in the most unique metaphors. I shared before; I got a river rock once during a group journey to the chamber. Everyone else came back describing these swords and shields, these beautiful and extravagant tools. I got some stupid rock. The value stems from the metaphorical meaning not the physical appearance. I treasure that river rock today and it is in the very bottom of my medicine bag. It is one of the few stones that I have which I do not allow anyone to touch. So when looking at what you receive it is vital to understand the deeper meaning, the metaphorical meaning.

Whatever the tool is that you will discover, you need to sit with it. Don't judge it. Spend time in meditation with it. After this first journey where you receive the gift, go back and ask your gatekeeper how to use it. Ask how to bring it back from the metaphorical to the practical. Let the tool share with you. If you get a river rock (my treasure from my first journey), go out and find a river rock and keep it. Hold it when you listen in meditation. Whatever your gift, find something in the physical that will represent the gift.

Before you begin your own journey, be sure to set your intention before you begin. Be open to receive whatever Spirit has to offer. Be open to the challenge it may bring. Be open to the metaphorical or symbolic.

CHAPTER 11

THE OUTER SPOKES

The Spokes of the Medicine Wheel are an inner journey through the mental, emotional, physical, and spiritual bodies. As each body is interrelated with another, there are times where they seem to flow into one another. When we sit down to truly contemplate our interrelatedness with those around us - not only with human beings, but with the animals, the plants, and the minerals of the earth - we begin to experience oneness.

The internal inventory and contemplation process takes as long as it takes. There are no set deadlines. There is no right or wrong way. I will share my journal entries with a spiritual mentor or teacher in order that I can see things from a sacred witness perspective. Be careful however, that as you do this walk, you do not fall into the seductive trap of morbid reflection. This is not a "beat up on you" walk. It is a journey to expose and reveal the authentic you. It is a journey to discover the things in YOUR life that causes barriers to YOUR growth. What do you need to let go of in order to receive new? Where have you made the greatest strides in your growth? What are your strengths that have formed the anchor for your foundation?

At birth, we are each given a beginning place upon the wheel; a specific direction to which we are born in. This starting point will guide us in our perceptions and actions throughout our lives. The true gift of life comes in when we walk the spokes and can receive the gifts of each direction to perceive life from. When we simply remain with the single perception we are not whole. We do not see in a holistic view point. The North gifts us, as example, wisdom. Without the gift of the South, one remains without emotion. The East shares vision, but without the West will not feel, nor experience unity with life. We learn our birth gift in the direction, but we must seek out and grow in understanding of all the directions if we wish to become whole and balanced in life. The compass guides us in this way.

As with any journey when things are uncovered and exposed, some things may sting and some things you will realize do not even belong to you and you now can return them to the rightful owner. If you approach this with an open mind, loving heart, pure intention and self-honesty, the results will be a deeper, enhanced relationship with all things.

CHAPTER 12

OUTER SPOKE EAST

Relatedness to Mother Earth

Virtue: Clarity

Intent: Seeing Beyond Self

Spirit of the East remind us of our Mother Earth and how she nurtures us so that we may nurture her.

The first outer spoke is focused upon Mother Earth herself. All of the gifts and life that she gives to us is the basis of all physical life. It is the creation deep within her core that offers the guidance and wisdom to each living being that lives upon her as well as feeling the imprints all living things leave upon her.

As you look upon the Mother Earth, the very basics of her nature is the soil. Is it simply dirt? Or do you see it as the foundation of life? The soil offers rich and precious gifts to every other kingdom that lives upon her surface.

There are many aspects to Mother Earth that can be contemplated. It truly is the core of the Sacred Web of the Middle World.

- What is your relationship with the soil of Mother Earth? Do you treasure it? Do you think about the compost that you make to add nutrients back into the soil? Do you treat it as though you are receiving a gift back? Or do you look at it as just dirt?

- What of the gems, rocks, and minerals that come from the Earth? Do you treasure them as sacred beings? Each stone has a voice, it has energy, and it has a vibrational frequency. Do you hear its message? Can you feel its living energy or do you see it just as a rock? Do you know where they came from? Were they taken from the Earth in a loving, sacred way? Or were they mined as though one were raping the Earth?

- Can you realize and experience that everything you touch, smell, see, feel and hear has its foundation in Mother Earth? Even the computer that you are reading this on and the chair you are sitting on all come from resources of Mother Earth. What are you doing today to treasure her? What imprint are you leaving on her and in the air that surrounds her?

- Do you reuse rather than buy new when you can? Do you recycle rather than throw away what you can? When cutting down a tree, do you renew by planting a new one in its place?

Can you see the interconnectedness and interrelatedness to all things upon the Earth. There are literally thousands of ways that you can honor and respect the Earth and all that she offers. When is the last time that you walked rather than drove your car? Stop and look at your own actions, look at the imprint they are leaving, and see if this is really the imprint you want your children to have to live with.

Imprints on Mother Earth Sacred Contract

I (add name), having fearlessly walked the Outer Spoke of the East and examined all the ways in which, in my life, Mother Earth has nurtured by being in this journey, and I now make sacred contract with Spirit of the East it to nurture Mother Earth and myself.

 In the presence of All My Relations, I firmly commit to the following Acts of Power: _____

I give myself permission to grow through each step in the living of my vision. Should I fail to honor my own commitment to this Act of Power, I agree to the giveaway of: _____

Sign and Date

When first developing your Acts of Power contracts it is best to begin with a single action you can do to empower yourself. Each contract and each giveaway will be unique to you.

So as you develop your power act and determine your giveaway, keep in mind the spoke you are working upon. An example of a power act can be to begin with picking up trash once a week on a hike to a local park. J a clean-up crew, or a personal and private contract. Or simply make a commitment once a week for a full year to go to a specific park and pick up the trash found.
The giveaway can be as simple as a crystal. Perhaps one you are physically attached to. If you do not fulfill your commitment, you promise to return the crystal to Mother Earth. Or perhaps give the crystal to someone who has no commitment or connection to Mother Earth. It is vital to understand the contract is a commitment to self and not to anyone else. While no one will know if you keep the contract – it is a sacred act that you are responsible for. It is a lesson in integrity, in ethics, and in commitment to self.

CHAPTER 13

OUTER SPOKE SOUTHEAST

RELATEDNESS TO 2 LEGGED (OR HUMAN)

Virtue: Innocence

Intent: Honor one another

The Two-Legged (or human) spoke is the next spoke of the Outer portion of the Medicine Wheel. This is the spoke in the Southeast of beginnings. The two-legged or the human's is about our attitude towards others. Please remember that this is about YOU and not others. This is about your thoughts, actions, and perceptions.

This spoke is about how we relate to self and others; with that being said, this is our first step in healing our own sacred being. Rather than give an expression of my opinions here, I will simply ask the questions. Be sure that you spend time diving into both sections separately. We do self-first and then others.

We begin with our attitude about ourselves. All attitudes, thoughts, actions and perceptions begin with those about our self.

- Do I consider myself as a Sacred being? How do I define what a Sacred being is?

- Do I treat myself as a Sacred being? Or do I mistreat myself with unhealthy lifestyle choices? Unhealthy relationships? What needs to change about the way that I treat myself?

- Do I nurture and love my own spirit, not just my physical body? What am I doing to nurture and love my spirit? When was the last time I had a belly laugh? A good cry? How much time do I spend nurturing myself? How much time do I spend meditating? How much time do I spend celebrating? Is this balanced?

- Do I seek out peace and harmony in my life? Or am I secretly seeking out drama? Do I strive to release and let go? Or do I cling and grasp tightly all that life gives?

- Do I treat each day as a sacred gift? Or am I wasting time like it is just always there? Do I celebrate the moments? Or am I waiting for the next moment?

Believe it or not, those were the easy questions. They only included self and the self-relationship. Now we look at our relationship with others. For each question above, we ask ourselves about others.

- Do I consider (family, friends, co-workers, people of other religions, people from other countries, of other economic classes, sexual preferences, and the list goes on and on – adapt to your life) to be Sacred beings? Or do I mistreat them with unhealthy lifestyle choices? Unhealthy relationships? What needs to change about the way that I treat others? What are my thoughts and emotions (which are the energy signatures that I am sending out) around each of these groups of people?

- Do I nurture and love their spirits, not just their physical body? What am I doing to nurture and love their spirits? When was the last time I shared a deep belly laugh? Shared a good cry? How much time do I spend nurturing others? How much time do I spend meditating and offering prayer for others? How much time do I spend celebrating other people's spirits and success? Is this balanced?

- Do I seek out peace and harmony in my relationships with others? Or am I secretly seeking out drama? Do I engage in others stories and make them my own? Do I enable others to remain in their drama and stories? Do I strive to release and let go? Or do I cling and grasp tightly all that life gives? Am I helping to perpetuate the drama with gossip and cutting tongue speech?

- Do I share examples with others through my action of how to treat each day as a sacred gift? Or am I sharing examples of how it is acceptable to waste time like it is just always there? Do I share examples of how to celebrate the moments? Or do I share examples of how I am waiting for the next moment? How tolerant of how others celebrate? Do I join them in celebrating?

These questions may sting as you read them and answer them honestly. This is not a process for those who do not wish to look at the shadow

123

aspects of their own spirit or become aware of defects within that need to be shifted. I can only assure you that as this walk continues, if you spend the time to reflect and contemplate the soul truth answers, the rewards of self-awareness are worth the effort.

NURTURING RELATIONSHIP SACRED

I (add name), having fearlessly walked the Outer Spoke of the Southeast and examined all the ways in which, in my life, my relationship with self and with others has nurtured by being in this journey, and I now make sacred contract with Spirit of the Southeast it to nurture all my relationships in life.

In the presence of All My Relations, I firmly commit to the following Acts of Power: _____

I give myself permission to grow through each step in the living of my vision. Should I fail to honor my own commitment to this Act of Power, I agree to the giveaway of: _____

Sign and Date

Begin by contemplating what a sacred relationship in your life looks like. What attributes of the relationship do you see as most valuable? Honesty, open communication, laughter, support, and balanced are a few of the single word attributes that might be on your list. Once having the list, then spend time looking at the closest relationships in your life (spouse, family, siblings, friends, etc) and ask yourself are you (not the other person) working towards these goals or away from them.

A sacred contract may be that you will hold yourself and all your relationships in a sacred container, with yourself working towards your ideal sacred relationship goals. This is highly valuable when you find yourself in situations with others that are not as harmonious as you would like. A giveaway here is a bit different as it is never punishment but rather energy exchange that is valuable. When you do not hold myself to the contract by seeing where you fell short of the ideal relationship, you may call or write the person and apologize for falling short in the relationship – regardless of whether you have the opinion it was not your responsibility. This does not mean that you do not hold the other person accountable; it simply means that you apologize for your part. There are times this is most difficult and there are times that after the action of extending an apology the relationship shifts – sometimes for the better and sometimes released. Remember, this is YOUR sacred contract, and what is offered is only examples of what you may consider.

CHAPTER 14

OUTER SPOKE SOUTH

RELATEDNESS TO SWIMMERS

Virtue: Growth

Intent: Discovery of self and purpose

As we continue the walk of the outer spokes, I
always have to pause each day and marvel at the
way nature seems to ensure that each day the
kingdom being reflected upon is shown in living
color. A blessing in focusing upon our awareness
of those things surrounding us is the moment our
eyes catch a hawk flying across the sky displaying
his glory or the incredible gentleness of the
manatee as it moves to the warm springs.

The Great Spirit paints masterpieces constantly
for us to enjoy. Do you realize how often do you
pause to notice them and speak your appreciation
to the Divine artist?

We are looking at our relationship with the
swimmers and the water they swim in. Your own
body is made up of a larger percentage of water –
and in some ways, as it seems all the spokes are,
this is a vital life giving relationship. Many will

relate to the dolphins, but what about the stingray or the shark? Every single swimmer must have our respect and honor – not only the pretty ones.

Questions for Journal Entry – Spoke South

- Turn your attention to those in the animal kingdom that swim or have fins. Consider not only the dolphins that share their message with us, but also the fish that we eat. Do you consider all of them sacred or only those of a beautiful and grand appearance? Do you thank the ones that give themselves to nourish my body as you eat them?

- What about the waters they live in? Do you practice conservation? Do you watch the products that you use in order to protect the waterways from chemicals? Do you participate in water cleanup? How do you feel about boating in waterways? What about the gasoline spilling into the waterways from the boat? Or the oil that gushes from wells? The spills? How do you feel about off shore drilling?

- What about the sea turtles, dolphins and manatees that are injured every year in boating accidents?

- Do you know what fish and finned animals are endangered? What about the whales being used for cosmetics? Do you purchase products that use animal fats and products? Do you participate in protecting our wetlands, ponds, and spawning grounds?

Water is essential to this kingdom. Water is also essential to your body. Do you see the interrelatedness and interconnection between yourself and the finned kingdom?

When was the last time that you paused and took notice of the condition of the waterway near your home? It is easy to ignore them when they are not visited.

Relationship with Water Sacred Contract

I (add name), having fearlessly walked the Outer Spoke of the South and examined all the ways in which the waters and all that swim in them has nurtured me by being in this journey, and I now make a sacred contract with Spirit of the South to nurture all my water relationships in life.

In the presence of All My Relations, I firmly commit to the following Acts of Power: _____

I give myself permission to grow through each step in the living of my vision. Should I fail to honor my own commitment to this Act of Power, I agree to the giveaway of: _____

Sign and Date

A sacred contract here may be spending time picking up trash on the waterways through a beach cleanup project. Or perhaps to honor the life giving water, build a rain water collection system. Conservation is a huge contract to fulfill. It takes time and effort and it is not convenient to water plants or wash vehicles without the pressure in a normal hose, however, it is important to our Mother Earth to conserve her resources.

CHAPTER 15

OUTER SPOKE – SOUTHWEST

Relatedness to Plants

Virtue: Sustainability

Intent: To contemplate internal belief
                systems

I spend much time in my gardens as the air around
me seems clearer and the energy brighter when I
am sitting in meditative reflection. In one of my
favorite gardens, a banana tree leaf covers and
shades me from the sun's rays as the roses waft
their aroma and the colors of the flowers fill my
vision. Many times as I sit in reflection, I will be
gifted with the sight of butterflies and
hummingbirds feeding on the nectar of the
flowers. It is a very serene and reflective
location. Do we consider the imprints we leave in
this kingdom and the medicine found here? When
I sit in this garden, the wheel becomes a living
breathing entity. It is easy to see how the plants
affect the animal world, my world and the world
of one another.

Last spring when I was in the middle of walking
my own wheel I had a huge lesson presented

which I am going to share here to show the lesson and sacred contract that was made.

I have an area that I call the nursery where plants are being started or need some extra tender loving care. It is more than a passion. It was shared with me a very long time ago from a mentor, if you want to get grounded the two easiest ways to do that are to clean your toilet or dig your hands in the earth. While the toilet must be cleaned, I find it much more enjoyable to dig my hands into the earth.

Spending some time in a front garden where the famous "stink weed" plant was growing rampant. The peeking of wild carrot and other blades of "weeds" were poking around the crocus. It can be a bit dangerous for me to weed, actually as I am highly allergic to the red ants that seem to be everywhere in Florida. It has been suggested that I wear long sleeves, high socks, and most definitely gloves when I garden. Of course, I cannot bring myself to wear gloves. The touch of the dirt against my fingertips just gives me goose bumps and transports me to another place.

So what is the lesson? I have often used the metaphor of weeding my garden for weeding the unwanted or no longer useful parts of life. With each blade pulled, I would visualize the pulling of something from my life (perhaps a bad habit or negative thought). This has always been my lesson in the gardens to look deeply within and what no longer serves me on my path today. This morning was different. I sat on the grass at first to just savor the warm rays of the sun beaming down. Inhaling deeply to breath all that fresh air into my lungs. Having not been out there for some time I was soaking it all in.

As I started to pull some of the stink weed from around a plant, I heard a distinct voice whispering "ouch". I stopped and looked around for a moment. Being that I often "hear" things, I had to make sure it was a whisper in the wind and not someone actually speaking. Shaking my head I began again to pull and tug at the difficult weed.

I often talk with my flowers as I am working in the gardens and today was no different. Well, it was different actually. I was cursing at the stink weed. "I have done everything to get rid of you. I burned you to send the signature out that you are not wanted. I have buried you. What do I have to do to make you stop growing in my garden?"

That is when it happened - the big "ahha" lesson. The "stink weed" started talking back. Then the birds started yelling and squawking. My quiet peaceful time in the garden was not to be. "Why are you trying to kill me?"

"You are a weed," I started in this long conversation with the stink weed.

"A weed to you, but not to all."

"I do not know a gardener that would call you anything but a weed."

"The creator does not make mistakes in what creates. I am only a weed because you say so. Do you not think that there is a purpose for all things?"

Gasp! A "stink weed" is going to give me a philosophical discussion on perspectives. This is so not going to happen. The weed is out of here was my thought. So I started tugging and pulling even harder and for some reason beyond my own understanding this particular strand I could not pull out of the ground. I sat back a bit frustrated.

I was forced to listen to the words in winds that the "stink weed" was speaking. The perspective of what I determine to be a weed and what the Creator determines to be a weed was shifting. It was only because I had a preconceived notion as to what the garden should look like that I deemed what was weed and what was not. As I sat there contemplating what was being shared, I was startled by a black racer snake. A rather large black racer. While they are not dangerous and are welcome in my gardens, the size startled me.

In total amazement and complete awe, I got to experience (for the first time I might add) a snake shedding its skin. As the snake slowly moved through the stink weed and crocus flowers it began to emerge from the skin. I dared not move fearing I would scare the beautiful renewal process. Mesmerizing is the only word I can use to describe. Once the process was complete and it did take some time, the whispers began again.

"There is a purpose to all things. A weed is only a weed because you perceive it to be so. This is true in your garden as it is in your life." Ouch!

Lessons can come from any place if only our hearts and souls are open to hearing them.

Questions for Journal Entry – Spoke Southwest

- Ask yourself if you treat the plants, flowers, and trees that surround you every day as sacred beings? They provide the clean air that you breathe and the beauty you enjoy. They give food and nutrients to both the animal kingdom and to you. Do you thank them for their endless giving?

- Do you think of the weeds you pull out? Do you see them as simply waste or do you see that they have hidden benefits? Dandelions grow in nearly every yard; do you remember that they provide nutrients valuable if you would pick them and put them in your salad. Some plants that we deem "weeds" offer soil nutrients for other flowers and plants. Do you simply discard them?

- Do you consider the effects of the chemicals used even on the side of roads that affect the plant kingdom? What else is affected by these chemicals? All in the name to "kill the weeds"? Do you support and eat organically grown foods without the harsh and sometimes toxic chemicals?

- What kind of fertilizer and chemicals are you using on your lawn to keep it the lush green that it is? Will they damage the soil that grows other plants? Will they damage the water?

- When was the last time that you went out and "hugged" a tree and felt the grounding life force energy that flows through it? What of the trees that are being cut down by the acres for development? How do you feel about that?

- What do you do to protect our environment from being paved over into parking lots? When planting, do you use hybrid seeds or natural seeds? Do you remember that the hybrid seeds are actually made by chemicals in factories and these seeds don't produce their own seeds?

- How long are you spending with your hands in the dirt speaking with the plants that live there? What are you growing in your gardens? Are you growing your own food or just the flowers for beauty? What is the real purpose of your gardens? Do you stand in awe of the beauty of creation as a bloom suddenly unfolds to reveal its flower?

The plant kingdom offers so much more than beauty. It provides food for both humans and countless kingdoms. It is vital that we stand vigilant in defense of the plant kingdom as it is being destroyed in order for human expansion. We must remember the interrelated dependence that exists.

There are locally owned organic farms in nearly every region. Discover one today and spend some time listening to the wisdom of the plants. Take a walk at a local park and pause to listen to the trees. Before picking food or flowers, pause and thank the plant for its bountiful gifts. Begin a small garden of your own and feel the depth of the connection. The vibrations of the plant kingdom can be heard if you stop, quiet yourself, and listen.

NURTURING PLANTS SACRED CONTRACT

I (add name), having fearlessly walked the Outer Spoke of the Southwest and examined all the ways in which the plants grow, how I nurture them and they nurture and support the world around me, and I now make a sacred contract with Spirit of the Southwest to nurture all my plant relationships in life.

 In the presence of All My Relations, I firmly commit to the following Acts of Power: _____
I give myself permission to grow through each step in the living of my vision. Should I fail to honor my own commitment to this Act of Power, I agree to the giveaway of: _____

Sign and Date

Set aside one garden area to grow as nature would have it. Allow it to wild with nature that it may be visited by frogs and snakes alike. Perhaps it maybe to create your own dirt from compost, or remove the flowers replacing with vegetables. The options for your contract are wild and open.

CHAPTER 16

OUTERSPOKE WEST

RELATEDNESS OF BUGS, SNAKES, AND LIZARD WORLD

Virtue: Experience

Intent: Introspection with open mind

This spoke reflects upon the bugs, snakes, lizards, or the creepie crawlies of the animal kingdom and they are not always what people wish to focus upon. I embrace the snake medicine as one of my totems. It was shared with me that the medicine of the snake is an allowance and permission (even perhaps a remembering) to "shake off" the confines of limitations and walls that I have carried within myself and in my life. This rawness can leave you literally feeling as though your entire being has been "shaken".

As we look at this kingdom, it is vital to keep an open mind. Snake medicine can mean many things. It is how the medicine is used as to what it means. It can be a transmutation and transformation of a being or a cycle of the being. It can be an initiation into another level of understanding and wisdom. It can be a venomous bite that can kill you if you do not become still and listen. Remember to this, every medical doctor wears two snakes on an emblem (embracing snake medicine on a whole new level).

Remember that a snake has the ability to go deep into Mother Earth on the physical level. The wisdom that snake medicine can provide can be the same. This means that it may be necessary when working with snake medicine to delve deep within you in order to discover the true aspects of the knowledge and wisdom being shared. So as I reflect on this kingdom, I remember to pause and look beyond the animal itself to what it can teach and share with me.

There are many oral stories about Grandmother Spider in various traditions. It is not always the biggest animal that carries the most powerful medicine. Consider as well the inter-relatedness of this kingdom to other kingdoms (as an example the bee medicine).

Questions for Journal Entry – Spoke West

- Do you consider the ants, snakes, lizards, spiders, frogs, and even the cockroaches being sacred beings?

- Do you think of the sacred interrelatedness between these creepie crawlies and the rest of the world? What lesson and wisdom is found in the red ants that bite and sting? What medicine does the spider share with you? Or the frogs? Have you considered that the cockroach is one of the most adept survivors in the entire animal world?

- Do you simply swat at a fly? When is the last time that you have sat and watched the fly; her habits and behaviors? What can you learn from the fly?

- What is the function and purpose of the bee? What is the real wisdom of their sting? When you put honey in your tea, do you pause to say thank you to the bees that provided it? What are your feelings on factory farming of honey bees?

- What is your thought of wearing skins of snakes? Crocodiles? Alligators? Do you use products made from these animals?

Every animal from the smallest to the venomous carries with it a message that has much wisdom to learn from.

Nurturing the Creepie Crawlies Sacred Contract

I (add name), having fearlessly walked the Outer Spoke of the west and examined all the ways in which the creepie crawlie relations nurture and the world around me, and I now make a sacred contract with Spirit of the west to nurture all my creepie crawlie relationships in life.

In the presence of All My Relations, I firmly commit to the following Acts of Power: _____

I give myself permission to grow through each step in the living of my vision. Should I fail to honor my own commitment to this Act of Power, I agree to the giveaway of: _____

Sign and Date

Most sacred contracts should be action items. Vowing not to use harsh chemical pest control opting only for natural deterrents is vital in keeping the balance of nature.
Treat things such as fleas with natural products such as Diatomaceous Earth. Many times the creepie crawlie relations are in the background of life, you can honor their path by committing to hours of community service behind the scenes. The thankless jobs that no one wants to do.

Remember as you create your power acts that it is highly personal but in your commitment focus upon the relatedness and relationship of the focus.

Meaning, if you are struggling to see what a giveaway might be - look at the medicine of the spoke and ask yourself how you can honor that.

CHAPTER 17

OUTER SPOKE– NORTHWEST

RELATEDNESS TO 4 LEGGED

Virtue: Equality

Intent: Walk My Talk

This is the spoke of the Northeast. The four-legged spoke is about our attitude towards animals with four legs including our pets and those that live in nature. Please remember that this is about YOU - your thoughts, your actions, and your perceptions.

There are many aspects of the four legged kingdom that need to be considered; however, this is about you. What are your feelings? How do you honor these animals? How you treat them as sacred beings? What can you do right where you are to help protect them?
We are all interrelated in the vast universe. We are interdependent with many in this kingdom. Think about your life as it would be if

suddenly there were no more cows on the Earth for example.

In many traditions the four legged world is revered and honored. Many of our sacred tools come from this kingdom; the skins of our drums or our hoofs on rattles are two examples, but there are many. Prophecies made on buffalo returning to the sacred cows in other lands all remind us of where our relationship to this kingdom should be.

Questions for Journal Entry – Spoke Northeast

- Let's first begin with our four legged pets. Those that we have in our homes, that we have brought into our families, from the dogs and cats to the mice some keep or the turtles – to cows and horses of the farms. Do you consider them to be sacred beings? It is easy to consider our own animals as sacred beings – but what of the ones we are not fond of? Are there those that we do not hold in divine love? Do you consider them as something less than a human friend? What about those that treat them as their children – do you hold them as spoiled animals or sacred beings? Do you care and nurture them as you do yourself or other 2 legged family members? Is the care balanced between the two? Do you treat your pets better than you do yourself? Why?

- What of other people's pets? Do you honor them as sacred? All breeds and types?

- Do you look at skunks and anteaters as sacred beings? Or do you treat some four legged animals as less valuable than others? A beautiful fawn walking in the morning mists is a sacred beautiful sight; what of a raccoon raiding your trash can? Do you look at the raccoon as a sacred being?

- Do you look at needing to give special care and nurturing to the four legged animals as humans take their homes in development? Do you take the time to think of their homes being lost when you cut a tree?

- What do you use and eat that is made from the four legged animal kingdom? Do you eat it with respect and honor? Do you treat that leather purse with great honor and respect for the animal that gave its life for your purse?

- What do you do to protect the homes and environment of those that our human society is destroying? Do you recycle? Conserve water? Replant?

- What of other places outside your own little community that are going through devastation like the rainforest? Do you even know what is happening? Do you know what animals are endangered because of the devastation? Why not?

The questions here are endless as one could take it from the physical world into the spirit world and back again only to scratch the surface of the inter relatedness and inter dependence of the two legged and four legged worlds.

4-LEGGED RELATIONS SACRED CONTRACT

I (add name), having fearlessly walked the Outer Spoke of the Northwest and examined all the ways in which the four legged relations nurture and the world around me, and I now make a sacred contract with Spirit of the Northwest to nurture all my four legged relationships in life.

In the presence of All My Relations, I firmly commit to the following Acts of Power: _____
I give myself permission to grow through each step in the living of my vision. Should I fail to honor my own commitment to this Act of Power, I agree to the giveaway of: _____

147

Sign and Date

From making a commitment to foster animals to speaking out against laws in support of the four legged kingdom are simple examples of this contract that can be made. It is important to remember that when making a sacred contract it should be something more than our natural way of being that we are agreeing to – something to allow the spirit to grow in understanding.

Remember, that as you make your contracts and consider your giveaways it is important that it is done with intent. This being a passion filled seeing our four legged relations as sacred beings; it shifts to intent of how can we honor and respect those relations.

It is important to remember that as we answer these questions, we are not having a "beat ourselves up" session. It is simply a time to contemplate and meditate where you are at the present moment and where you wish to go in the future. If you do not have a book mark of how far you have come, it is impossible to look at your own progress. The reflections and shifts of awareness that occur during the walking of the spokes can cause a range of emotions to crop up. They can range from how far you have come, to how far you still need to go in order for that idealistic goal to be achieved. Each question reveals awareness of what areas that are still lacking in wisdom or strength.

It is also important to remember, this is a journey. It is not a race. You may feel compelled to remain on a previous spoke for multiple weeks. This will become even more prevalent when we begin the inner spokes which will dive deeper into the waters of our inner relationships with self. Dissecting our code of ethics and moral codes can bring up many emotions. It is vital to remember that the intent, the purpose of walking the medicine wheel is for healing, for clarity, and for evolvement of the spirit.

CHAPTER 18

OUTER SPOKE – NORTH

RELATEDNESS TO WINGED

Virtue: Cleansing

Intent: Renewal

The outer spoke of the North focuses upon the winged ones that fly across the skies. I remember having a defined definition of flying animals while I was walking the wheel one fall. I had to do some research for something related to snake medicine. The link I stumbled upon was for snakes that fly. There is actually a particular type of snake in Asia that flies or glides nearly 330 feet from branch to branch. It reminds me that anything is possible. It also shows me that the interrelated threads that weave through the Web of life are defined only by my terms, not by the animals' terms, nor the Universal Consciousness' terms.

Questions for Journal Entry – Spoke North

- Ask yourself if you consider all winged animals as being sacred beings (Including the mosquitoes that bite and love bugs that cover our cars here in Florida)? Do you think about the sacredness of the turkey as you sit down at the table on Thanksgiving and give thanks that he gave a life to nourish your body?

- How do you feel about the ones that are caught for domestication and caged? Or the ones in the zoos in cages? These are wild animals that we as humans have determined to keep for ourselves; how do you feel about that?

- What about the animals raised solely for our food? How do you feel about how the chickens are raised for eggs or our cookouts?

- What about the oil spills? What is your feeling on the devastation to the birds themselves and to their homes they live in? The oil spills are not the only thing taking their homes away. What about the loss of woods where they live?

- How do you feel about mosquito control with chemicals?

- When was the last time you sat down outside to watch the winged kingdom? Have you ever watched a hummingbird drink the nectar from a flower and realized how the flowers and trees are interrelated in the cycle of life?

- Have you ever just sat and watched the migration of birds? How incredible the flight plan is? Watched a vulture disappear into the clouds and then fly straight down to the ground at an incredible speed, never slowing, simply grasping its food and flying straight back up? How about a bird diving for a fish from the sky? How they are able to see beneath the surface where the fish is from a height high enough that their shadow does not scare the fish?

The butterfly is an amazing winged animal, as is the eagle and peacock, but the stinging bee, pesky love bugs, and mosquitoes are just as sacred. Can you see the medicine in the not so popular winged ones?

What of the feathers that come from the birds? Many times these are used in sacred objects. When you find feathers how do you honor the bird that gifted them for your object?

Winged Relations Sacred Contract

I (add name), having fearlessly walked the Outer Spoke of the North and examined all the ways in which the winged relations nurture and the world around me, and I now make a sacred contract with Spirit of the North to nurture all my winged relationships in life.

In the presence of All My Relations, I firmly commit to the following Acts of Power: _____
I give myself permission to grow through each step in the living of my vision. Should I fail to honor my own commitment to this Act of Power, I agree to the giveaway of: _____

Sign and Date

One may nurture and foster wild birds on your property to going to the Gulf during the oil spill crisis to spend time assisting in the cleanup. Perhaps it is to honor the feathers found in special ceremony as a medicine act to creating habitat on your property for hummingbirds and butterflies.

Remember we do not walk these spokes perfectly. Yet, it is absolutely vital when you are making your sacred contracts (including your giveaways) that when you fall short, you keep your contract with the spirit world. It is your integrity. If you are not willing to follow through with your contract's giveaway – please do not make the contract. Consider your words carefully. If you keep the contract, follow the giveaway when you fall short, the Spirit world will see your words and actions meet and gift you far more than you can imagine.

CHAPTER 19

OUTER SPOKE – NORTHEAST

RELATEDNESS TO UNIVERSE

Virtue: Honesty

Intent: Live in Light of Truth with
Integrity

We find ourselves standing at the gateway of the Northeast. It is a gateway to the Universe; for some, the most difficult of all the spokes thus far, for others the beginning of the journey.

What does it mean to be related to the Universe, the Cosmos, and the Source? What does it mean to even say that a Divine reality within the Cosmic Universe exists? The truth of our origins, of our understanding, of our source lie within this spoke. It is where we seek the answer to the implication of considering that there is more to the universe than the moon and stars in the skies. It is where we consider the implications of the existence of realms not visible, not seen, but always known.

This is a spoke of truths within; yet, in some ways this spoke can never be fully understood until we find ourselves on the "other side" of the spoke. There is much to learn from our own limited understanding.

This spoke looks at our relatedness of the Sun. The moon. The stars. The Heavens. It is a spoke many become lost within the questions never finding the answers. It is imperative to dive deep yet consistently break the surface for breaths of air. This spoke prepares us for the spiral inward to begin the walk of the inner spokes. There are more questions that have only your truths for answers.

Questions for Journal Entry – Spoke Northeast

- What effect does the sun have upon our lives?

- What about the moon and its effect upon the tides and your emotions?

- Do the stars have an effect? What about the new stars coming into our immediate cosmos?

- How do you feel about the space 'junk' left behind?

- What about our atmosphere? How do you feel about pollution?

- Have you ever thought about the relatedness of the air you breathe every day?

- Do you see the interrelatedness of the 'local' universe with all other kingdoms? When is the last time that you sat outside and looked up at the stars?

- The 'local' universe versus the 'cosmic' universe is a deeper understanding.

- What are your thoughts on other realms?

- Do you journey or perhaps see and hear spirit guides? Where do they come from? How can you see or hear something that is not there? Is it real?

- What about angels?

- Is there something after physical death? Where do they come from?

- Can you see your place in the 'local' universe? The 'cosmic' universe?

The result of pausing here to openly and trustingly go into deep journeys can result in a small, but deep understanding of your inter-relatedness to the Cosmic Universe. These are questions that will continue on for a life time and beyond. We will go deeper with this relatedness, this relationship, on the inner spokes, the Center Hub, and once more in the Great Mystery.

Relationship with the Universe Sacred Contract

I (add name), having fearlessly walked the Outer Spoke of the Northeast and examined all the ways in which the Universe, the Cosmos, the Divine and I are related, and I now make a sacred contract with Spirit of the Northeast to nurture my relatedness with the Universal Cosmos in life.

In the presence of All My Relations, I firmly commit to the following Acts of
Power: _____
I give myself permission to grow through each step in the living of my vision. Should I fail to honor my own commitment to this Act of Power, I agree to the giveaway of: _____

Sign and Date

This is a highly personal (more than other spokes) Sacred Contract. One that requires deep commitment to the journey. It is here that many become lost and do not continue the walk of the spokes.

When making this contract, go back and consider the Universe as it relates to the other outer spokes. How does the Universe relate to the Animal kingdoms, the plant kingdoms, the minerals and rocks, and the two legged relations? As I shared early on in this book, when learning the gift of the wheel it was done through the use of spirit lodges for journey's to deeply understand each spoke. Sit facing the northeast and look to the east of this lodge to look at the relationship and relatedness of the Universe and our Mother Earth; then look the southeast to reflect the 2 legged, the south and swimmers, the southwest and plants, the west and creepie crawlies, the northwest and the 4 legged, the north and the winged, and finally look back the northeast to contemplate upon your journey.

The commitment for this spoke is one to continue to the inner spokes. To continue the spirit lodges. To continue the walk. To continue regardless of the cost. Sounds melodramatic, but here is where you make your commitment to Creator to do the pictures even when you do not understand them, to live your code, and to stand in your truths.

As you reflect upon your own contract, consider the past few months. Consider what you have uncovered and discovered about yourself and ask yourself the question. Are you willing to continue? How does the universe support you? How are you giving thanks to the Universe for supporting you? If you were standing face to face with the Creator of the Universe, what would you say? How would you show your humble appreciation for the gifts received?

CHAPTER 20

OUTERSPOKE CONCLUSION

If you are looking for more to do remember that with each spoke you can go back to it and sit in your spirit lodge in a different place to get a different perspective. What I mean is - let's say you are called to the swimmers. You go to the south and rather than seeing the questions from the south, sit in the north seat of the south direction. How does the swimmers and the winged ones relate to one another? Or move to the northwest and see how the swimmers are related to the 4 legged of our world? How are they interdependent upon one another?

The wheel is never ending. There are many aspects that one could approach to see a new perspective from, that approach is the journey and lasts a life time. The wheel is a living, constantly moving energy. It is not something simply to be done, but it is how to live life.

As we approach the inner spokes, take a moment and revisit your sacred contracts. Pick a word or two from each spoke and draw your medicine wheel. On each outer spoke write the words. This gives you the threads of your new tapestry to begin weaving.

CHAPTER 21

THE INNER SPOKES

The intention of the inner spoke walk is to discover truth. We will be walking to answer the questions of:

- Who am I
- Why am I here
- What is my purpose
- Where did I come from
- Where am I going
- How do I get there

Big questions that come with deep answers that each one will discover differently as there is no right or wrong truths. We will journey together to asses ourselves and consider various perspectives in order to realize the truth within ourselves. Once we discover the truth by determining what the illusion was, we will work on clearing the illusion through ritual action, sacred contracts, and journal work so that we may see our authentic self.

We will dive in to look at our perceptions, how we trust, what we believe, and why we believe it. We will see what our relationships are and how we sabotage ourselves. How we leak and give away our power, what our integrity really looks like and how our stories really are written. This is a process that at times will reveal the best of who we are and at others the worst of who we are. But it is imperative that we remember that in discovering the worst is what the richest compost of life is made from.

Going backwards In order to propel forward.

We walked the outer spokes of the wheel which revealed our relatedness with all that is outside of us. Our relationship with the 4 legged, the swimmers, the plants, the creepies, the winged ones, with Mother Earth and even the Universe. We have begun to see how every choice we make in life leaves an imprint. We were reminded to walk softly. Now we learn to walk with assurance.

As we transition, one quote comes to mind "no one is an expert on the human experience". The human experience is about movement, in thought, and in form. It is about movement within thought, movement within form, thought behind movement, thought form, and even movement in form. The journey here is of the mental, emotional, physical, and spiritual bodies interwoven as one whole being. Each of the bodies is interrelated to another and flow energetically with one another.

- There is no right or wrong way to do the journey.
- The only vital piece is the honesty you gift yourself during the journey.
- Remember at times we can perceive thoughts, actions or emotions so that our own objectivity is lost.
- Do not get lost in morbid reflection. This is not a beat up on you journey. It is a journey to expose the authentic you.

This discovery, this accounting of your spiritual nature will expose many things, some may sting when brought into the open. Your suitcase will be opened so that all those "items" that do not even belong to you are given back to the rightful owner. A spiritual accounting must be done with an open mind, loving heart, and complete honesty. The result – an enhanced, deeper relationship with yourself, with others, and with Divine Source.

As you purify and prepare for the second leg of our journey, ask in your meditations and prayers that you be graced with an open mind, loving heart, and self-honesty. Ask that all which needs to be revealed is exposed.

In the preceding chapters on the outer spokes, many suggestions were given for your acts of power and give away. As you have become accustom to creating these acts of power, in the inner spokes we will lay the responsibility upon yourself to complete your own power acts.

EXERCISE: MEDICINE BAG

The medicine bag will be representative of our work on the inner spokes and central hub of the wheel. Within it will be a personal and sacred representation of your contract, your lesson, or your medicine from each spoke. This is a personal and sacred creation. The bag can be an elaborate leather pouch or a simple piece of cloth that you place your sacred items in. The important focus here is not on the bag itself, but the sacred intent of your creating it yourself. This is not something you will go out and purchase. It is something you must make yourself. (My first bag was a piece of cloth tied with twine – the twine had a couple of feathers found during the journey around the wheel – it does not have to be elaborate. Find your bag that you will hold all the items from the walk.

As we have walked the outer spokes of the wheel which has been all about our relatedness with that which is outside of us, we have looked at how we are related to all humans, to the 4 legged world, the swimmers, the plants, the creepies, the winged ones, the Universe and with Mother Earth herself. We have begun to see how every choice we make leaves an imprint. We remember to walk softly and with assurance.

As we transition to walk the inner spokes, one quote comes to mind "no one is an expert on the human experience." The human experience is about movement, and thought, and form. It is about movement within thought, movement within form, thought behind movement, thought form, and even movement in form. The inner spokes are truly an inward journey of mental, emotional, physical and spiritual bodies. Each body interrelated to another and flowing energetically into one another.

In the preceding chapters on the outer spokes, many suggestions were given for your acts of power and give away. As you have become accustom to creating these acts of power, in the inner spokes we will lay the responsibility upon yourself to complete your own power acts.

Again, there is no right or wrong way to walk the inner spokes. The vital piece is the honesty you gift yourself in the walk. At times we can perceive things so that our own objectivity is lost. Be careful if you take this journey not to spend time in a morbid reflection. This is not a beat up on you journey. It is a journey to expose the authentic you. To discover the things that can cause barriers to your growth? What are the things that you need to release in order to receive new abundant gifts? Where have you made great strides in your growth? What are the strengths that have held your foundation?

An accounting of your spiritual nature will expose many things, some of which may sting as you see them, perhaps for the first time, for what they really are. While other things you may come to realize do not even belong to you and must be given back to the rightful owner. If this is done with an open mind, loving heart, and complete honesty, the results will enhance your relationship with self, others, and with a Divine Source.

The mantra here is to speak your truth to yourself.

CHAPTER 22

INNER SPOKE – EAST

TRIBE

Virtue: Perception

Intent: Discovering Who Am I

The East is about discovering who you are and what your self-truths are. It is difficult to see oneself with complete honesty. Many times we do not even realize that we are wearing a mask. Until we have that moment of illumination and see our true selves for the first time, we believe the illusion; we believe the mask reflected is our true self.

This is truly the beginning of the journey. The beginning of knowing who you are, what you believe and how you act. The mask is all about perception. Our perception of self begins with how we see others, how we interact with others and how we behave with others. When the mask is removed we realize in truth we are all one; however, getting to that knowledge and knowing it can be a difficult prospect.

We are very much like standing at the front door to our inner temple working to have a spiritual cleanup that we may be cleansed to enter. The goal of this spoke is to finally be able to stand and speak truths about self to self. As we look to the foundation of our self, we begin with looking to our tribes. Where we built our foundation, our beliefs, and our truths. It is in looking to these relations that we can begin to discover the masks we have picked up. We look to our behaviors, our perceptions, our emotions, and our actions; we are not looking at how others behave, feel, or act.

Questions for Journal Entry – Inner Spoke - East

We begin with the tribe.

- What is your definition of your tribe?

- What is your relationship with your tribe? A tribe is your family, your community, your co-workers. For each of these 'tribes' ask yourself:
  - What is the relationship that I currently have?
  - What hinders these relationships?
  - Do I hold any old belief patterns from these relationships? Do I hold resentment, guilt, shame, or fear in any of these relationships? Is there anger within these tribes?

As you are asking yourself these questions about your tribal relationships, when finding that there is resentment or shame (for example), spend some time writing about that situation.

- What caused it? Remember this is your journey not that of someone else's, so as you write, write about your part, your feelings, your understanding, and what you would have like to have had happen. Don't worry about the other person or persons.

- With the members of my tribe, are there areas that I have been self-centered, selfish, or self-seeking that caused any of these issues? What areas of my life are being affected because of these issues? What are the old belief patterns that I learned from my tribe that are no longer useful and need to be let go of? What values or principles are affected?

When we look at the tribe it is the basis of our foundation in life. It is where most of our values and principles came from. Many times as we become awakened and we look back, we find that the blocks within even our energy systems are a result of situations that go back to our tribal times.

In spending time to clear this inner part of our life, we not only clear the energy surrounding our beliefs of the tribal life, but we can see where our new tribe can be shifted when we see it from a new perspective.

How many times have you heard people talk about their childhood with some sarcasm or negative connotation? This is a result of not letting go of things that are no longer working in our lives. This is true even of our work situation and in our communities. If the trait exists in our tribal family, it also exists in our work relationships and our community relationships.

This is the spoke that most have the hardest time with. Many issues arise and cause emotional pain that tells us I do not need look back there again and we continue denying ourselves the freedom of release that happens in going through the process.

The thought of this spoke is that we are all one. That we are all interconnected with one another and with life. As we look at that thought, we understand the relationship with our biological family. We also must understand that we are all part of one Divine family. One tribe. To fully understand and accept that we are all one tribe is a spiritual challenge that faces every one.

- Who do you consider your Tribe? Do you feel more, or less connected with people through this vehicle of social media? Does it feel like rich connections with depth? Does it surprise you to be able to connect deeply with people this way? I've been really thinking about how this 'energy' seems to be 'felt' somehow through these social media connections

- So I ask as a different aspect of this walk, how is the internet affecting your "tribe"? Are the relationships here as real and authentic as other "traditional" relationships? Is the male energy not being felt? Do you consider your social media "tribe" part of your real tribal family? Has this Internet family enhanced or hurt your physical tribal family? Does it feel like rich connections with depth? Does it surprise you to be able to connect deeply with people this way?

Defining Self

Can you define who you are? Begin with writing ten strengths and 5 weakness from the answers written to your journal questions.

Can you see the shadow in the weaknesses such as fear of abandonment?

Now go out in nature, smudge yourself and dig a hole. As you dig a hole focus upon the shadow aspects discovered, the weakness uncovered, and the mask removed. All that wish to cleanse and release.

Now lay on your belly so that your entire being is as close to Mother Earth as possible and speak into the hole. Speak what you are cleansing and releasing. Speak your truths discovered whether you wish to shift them or not – at the moment they are your truths. Speak them all into the hole.

Inhale deeply and blow all the feelings, all the pent up emotions, into the hole. Give it all be it anger, frustration, or gratitude and love. While still on belly add flowers, cornmeal, or whatever natural gift you brought with you to represent your gratitude and place in the hole.

Cover the hole and speak words of gratitude to Mother Earth for taking your truths and transforming the energies into love, compassion, and gratitude.

It is impossible to follow a code of ethics when you have no idea how to have a healthy connection with others. The results of not having healthy relationships are guilt and shame over the consequences of your own actions or non action as the case may be. Almost worse than the harm that may have been cause to those around us with actions, a person further harms themselves with heavy handed embarrassment, guilt and shame.

Attitude changes are required to happen before any actions to rid yourself of all this guilt. Everyone deserves to live guilt and shame free. There is a way out from it. The first step is taking responsibility for those things that you have done to create the guilt and shame in the first place. To take responsibility means that you have discovered what your own set of ethics are. This is a huge step in being able to release yourself from the clutches of the guilt. The process of taking responsibility can be empowering. Once you have taken personal responsibility of your own actions, you can begin once more to show care and concern. First to yourself and then to others by having the readiness to take a change in your actions. During this process you will begin to see a change or shift in your perceptions.

When you begin to take responsibility rather than simply dwelling in the shame, the ghosts of your past will start to disappear. As these ghost disappear your self-worth will increase. You deserve to live guilt free. It is self-destructive to continue to punish yourself by holding onto the guilt of the past. To continue the action required to achieve this new way of living requires some courage and determination. It is not enough to take personal responsibility within yourself, you must take it one step further.

This means going to those about you that are in direct relation to where the guilt source is. This is a difficult task. However, this is paramount to realize the full gift of living completely guilt free in your life. When living in this state of mind of constant guilt and shame, the life is chaotic catching everyone around in a vortex of craziness. Stepping outside the vortex and simply stating your part (your responsibility) can stop the vortex not only for you, but for the others in your life. The choke hold of guilt will loosen with each step you take in making amends for your actions. Facing the reality of your actions breaks the cycle of guilt. Guilt is a powerful and destructive force that persists and grows left unchecked.

To deal with such a powerful force, you absolutely need a powerful and drastic action. That powerful action comes from your willingness to take deliberate actions in your life today to free it from any guilt or shame you have held onto. Life will take on a new meaning and new experience. Going to the people whom you hurt by your actions and taking responsibility does so much more than making peace with them. It frees you in a way that you cannot even fathom until you experience it.

When you are able to take such responsibility for your own actions, you will begin to truly connect with yourself and others in a healthy way. The re connection will tap into an inner resource with in you that you never knew was there. This inner resource allows you to find and maintain a sense of wholeness. A wholeness that is secure. You will have blessings come to you in the most unlikely circumstances when you are able to release yourself from the clutches of guilt and be truly free.

When you cannot go directly to the person, for whatever reason (including self-protection or harmful repercussions to yourself or others), the action of placing those names into the hole is a powerful statement to the Universe and can assist you in the freeing of guilt.

Universal Tribe Sacred Contract

I (add name), having fearlessly walked the Inner Spoke of the East and examined my self-truths and my tribes, I now make a sacred contract with the Universal Tribe.

In the presence of All My Relations, I firmly commit to the following Act of Power: I will see myself honestly. I will act in my truths honestly. I will speak my truths honestly.

I give myself permission to grow through each step in the living of my vision. Should I fail to honor my own commitment to this Act of Power, I agree to the giveaway of:_____

Sign and Date

CHAPTER 23

INNER SPOKE – SOUTHEAST

Relationships Ancestors to Now

Virtue   Respect

Intent   Return to Innocence

As we continue our walk of the inner spokes, this spoke focuses on Relationships. Whether you are in a relationship with a partner or it is a relationship with co-workers, we all have relationships. The one most ignored is the relationship with self. In order to have a balanced relationship with others, you must have an intimate relationship with self. The other relationship we tend to ignore is the relationship with our ancestors. We look at the relationship with ancestors many times as simply a remembering rather than an active engagement. This spoke also focuses on your creative abilities in your relationships.

This is the spoke of our stories. We often talk about dropping the stories in order to see from a different perspective. Here we step into the stories of our relationship patterns, our inheritance suitcase. The stories are where our belief systems have been created. Those beliefs begin with our relationships. How have the relationships developed, where have our stories disempowered ourselves and others, and what does the stories tell us about our ability to become the sacred witness who stands in innocence without prejudgment.

If we see our life as a stage, and we can sit in the audience without becoming drawn in to the characters, we can begin to see where the patterns are, the origin of our strengths and weaknesses, and our ability to speak our authentic truths. It is within this spoke that we define our ideal relationship and our code of honor. We are going to look at current relationships, however, this spoke can go deep into the patterns, beliefs, and relationships of our ancestors. It is one, in my opinion, of the most important spokes to work on and one of the most difficult.

Questions for Journal Entry – Inner Spoke – Southeast

- When was the last time you treated yourself as Divine? Can you be completely honest in defining how you wish to be treated? Or do you exaggerate things to make yourself seem better than…?
- Where do you get your self-identity from?

- Do you consider yourself a creative being? How do you express your creativity?

- As this is a partnership spoke, are you comfortable with your sexuality? Do use your sexuality as a power tool or a blaming tool?

- Are you strong enough and balanced enough to honor your own set boundaries?

- Do you have a personal code of honor? Do you stand firm in it or do you negotiate it with yourself to meet other people's expectation?

- Do you allow fear to dictate your choices rather than mastering your fears? Are you self-justifying your fears? Rationalizing them?

- What goals do you have for yourself? In relationships? In career? In spiritual growth?

- Are you in an ideal relationship with yourself and others? Have you defined

what your ideal relationship is? Not only
a partnership/love relationship – but every
relationship that you have – how do they
measure to your ideal relationship? How
do you measure yourself against this ideal
relationship?

- How do you see your relationship with
  your ancestors? How do you honor that
  relationship? How do you wish the
  generations after you to see you as an
  ancestor? Do you go to the spirit world
  for wisdom? Do you listen or really hear
  the wisdom from the ancestors? Do your
  actions reflect the wisdom you have been
  given in all aspects? Do you just share the
  wisdom from the elders to sound wise or
  do you actually apply it in your own walk?

This spoke is about honoring self and
others. Honoring self allows us to cherish the
sacred relationships we have with others. How
you respond to others is based upon how you
respond to yourself. You are a sacred being.

INHERITANCE SUITCASE

Define five beliefs or patterns that you are
grateful that were gifted by your parents. Define
five beliefs or patterns that you see as
weaknesses. Look at both and see where your

parents learned the patterns from. Can you see why your parents did or believed as they did? Look at your lists and determine what you wish to shift and what you wish to

Write a story that is about what you wish to release in 3-5 paragraphs. Then rewrite the story with the beliefs that you will strive to live in the future based upon your strengths. Take the story you wish to release to the fire using the affirmation I heal my stories through universal power of love, compassion and forgiveness.

IDEAL RELATIONSHIP

Looking back to your journal entries and make a list of what your ideal relationship looks like. This is a list for all relationships not simply for partnership. For example:

Ideal list: Honest, open communication, balanced decision making, laughter might be things on your list. Keep this list and as you become aware of confrontation or frustration in any relationship, ask yourself am I being honest, am I having open communication, am I balancing decisions with my compromising ability, or am I gifting moments of laughter in the relationship. This is about you and where you are falling short in the relationship. It allows you to see yourself honestly without opinion about another's actions.

UNIVERSAL CONSCIOUSNESS SACRED CONTRACT

I (add name/spirit name), having fearlessly walked the Inner Spoke of the Southeast and examined myself truths about my ancestors and my own stories, I now make a sacred contract with the Universal Consciousness.

In the presence of All My Relations, I firmly commit to the following Act of Power: My Code of Honor
My relationship code of honor is:
a.
b.
c.
d.
e.
f.

I will respect self and others by:
        a.
        b.
        c.

I will shift the following belief patterns to (from your goals list in the journal entry):
      Belief   Shift to
1.
2.
3.

I give myself permission to grow through each step in the living of my vision. Should I fail to honor my own commitment to this Act of Power, I agree to the giveaway of:_____

Sign and Date

CHAPTER 24

INNER SPOKE – SOUTH

PERSONAL POWER

Virtue: Trust
Intent: Why am I here?

As we continue our walk of the inner spokes, this spoke focuses on our own personal power. This is the power that makes us an individual with personality and how we relate to the external world specifically how we honor ourselves. There are different variations of this power to consider. Finding your own voice to speak what personal truths are. Having the internal stamina to preserve through the mental and emotional aspects of life; having the backbone so to speak to stand up for self. Finally, the evolution of growth mentally, emotionally, and spiritually is part of the personal power. This is one of the most difficult spokes to walk and remain open, honest, and sincere as you ask yourself the questions. It can cause a great deal of emotional upheaval. To be sure though, the rewards are great in coming to discover your true nature.

- Do you honor yourself as a sacred being? (Not do we treat ourselves as sacred; but rather do we HONOR ourselves)

- Do you love yourself at the core?

- Do you even like yourself? If you don't, why not?

- What is it that you don't like specifically?

- Are you changing what you don't like about yourself?

An exercise to work with for the above questions is to sit down and write a list of 10 things you absolutely love about yourself and 5 things that you would like to change. This process sometimes of simply making a list can help facilitate the answers to the above.

- Are you honest? With yourself? With others?

- Do you exaggerate the truth to make yourself look better to others? To justify or rationalize your reactions? Why? To you misrepresent the truth to down play your own actions? Why?

- Are you critical of other people and their actions?

- Do you blame others to justify your own reactions?

- Do you hide behind the rationalization that at least I didn't do what (insert name) did?

- Why are you trying to protect yourself?

- Can you admit to being wrong? Can you let others give you feedback when you are wrong?

- Can you accept approval and recognition from others gracefully? Or do you shy away from it? Why? Or do you feel the need to seek out others approval to feel worthy?

- Do you consider yourself to be strong? List three strengths. Do you consider yourself to be weak? List three weaknesses.

- Do you fear taking care of yourself and depend on someone else to do it for you?

- Are your relationships healthy or are you in them simply because you are afraid of being alone?

- Do you respect yourself? Or do you treat yourself in a manner that you would not allow others to do?

- Can you stick to a decision to change your life or do you give up easily?

- What about responsibility? Are you responsible for yourself? Or do you feel like you have to be responsible for everyone in your life?

- Do you want to change something about your life? Or simply resigning yourself to living the life you have been? Make a list of 10 things you absolutely love about your life and 5 that you wish to change. The five you wish to change write a couple of sentences that give you an idea of what you need to do to change it and start applying them one at a time.

If you have answered the questions truthfully and completely, you will have discovered some big chunks about which you are and what needs to change to become the person you want to be. This process can be difficult as many have not taken an honest look at themselves. You may wish to speak with someone about what you have discovered on this spoke. If you have a spiritual teacher explain to them what you have done, they will be happy to help you on your path of evolution.

POWER LEAK DISCOVERY

Your thoughts are affected by your attitude. Your attitude is affected by the people you surround yourself with. Mental attitude will be positive if you are with positive can-do attitude rather than those who have a negative, it is all too difficult, why bother attitude. When a person can maintain a positive attitude they will find that they have a higher level of energy thus allowing them to have a greater degree of personal power. Positive attitude's lead to finding interesting opportunities that can benefit everyone around you. With this attitude, mountains will turn into molehills; whereas, a negative attitude can cause you to have major setbacks.

Personal power comes through positive mental attitude. When a positive attitude is in place it attracts others who can help them, it attracts people with solutions to problems, and it will develop and strengthen your own personal power ultimately leading to your own success. Anyone has the ability to tap into the power of a positive attitude. With persistence and effort you can gradually change your thoughts into predominantly positive ones.

The process of change is not as daunting as it may seem. The first step to understanding how personal power works is to step back and watch yourself and the events as they unfold. Try to determine what attitude you are having in any given situation. It may be helpful to write down each night the events of the day and in a column next to it write down what attitude you had during the event. When you have an event in black and white on a piece of paper it is easier to look back objectively at how you handled the situation.

The real key is to add the third column. This is how to develop your own personal power. Write down the ways you could have handled the situation in a more positive light. This will allow you to see where changes are needed. By keeping a record it allows you to see the progress you are making.

As days unfold, begin to work on the areas you have identified in your inventory. You will see the amazing difference small changes are having in tapping into your own personal power. Having the ability to look at your mind set on paper enables you to understand in a completely objective way what your strengths and weaknesses are. This is the secret to understanding your personal power and making it work for you.

DESIRE, DREAM, AND YOUR DESTINY

To discover your destiny, your purpose here must begin with the small pieces which when put together reveal the big picture. We begin the discovery process by simply making a decision to let the eternal fire within that will ignite your authentic voice – your destiny. The small pieces are your desires. The ideas and thoughts of what you desire at this particular moment.

What is a desire really? It is an energy force that propels your dreams. It is an emotional energy that connects your thoughts with your soul. The difficultly with desire is becoming stuck in always having a desire and not allowing the energy to propel you.

EXERCISE: DREAM AND DESIRE

Close your eyes for a moment and begin to see a golden sunrise. Focus on the golden color for a few minutes basking in the warmth as you breath the color within. Allow it to fill you. When you are ready ask yourself the simple question if you knew there were no limitations, no boundaries in life, what would you do? Sometimes desires are clear and other times they seem so distant we cannot access them, cannot identify them. If this is the case, repeat the exercise and find something small that you desire – perhaps 10 minutes to go for a walk in nature, or perhaps you wish to be of service you just don't know how. Find a small desire that you can fulfill easily and begin there. Taking that small desire and fulfilling it begins the process of igniting the energy again. It will start the motion of propelling you forward in your desires. There is a saying that when you live life to the fullest every moment of the day, you create a world full of life.

What about seeing desires that are perhaps not for our higher good or towards fulfilling our purpose? Each of us has a hunger within us that will reveal desires which have motive. These are not always negative or positive in nature but they do contain self. Self-desires are simply a way to fill a void within; gratification of self. When you do the above exercise, write down the desires that you discover. Going through the list ask yourself how the desire makes you feel, does it impact self and the world positively, and do I need to call upon the spirits to help me fulfill. Does the desire have a basis from being hurt in the past, does it only serve to show I am good enough in the world, or does it need approval from someone in the physical world? These answers will reveal to you whether the desire is working towards your purpose. Discovering the intention energy of the desire is what helps one discover if it is a destiny desire or a gratification desire. This is an exercise in self-honesty.

Dreams. Moving a desire to a dream is simply an exercise in energy. Once we have discovered some basic desires, we can then begin to paint the canvas of dreams. It is important here to state a goal and a dream are not the same thing. Goals are the action of how to achieve; while dreams are what we wish to achieve. Dreams will challenge you to use your personal power and connect you with your spirit.

EXERCISE: DISCOVERING YOUR DREAMS.

Ask yourself:

- When was the last time in this life that you truly felt exhilarated and fulfilled?
- When was the last time in this life that you felt creative in any manner?
- When was the last time in this life that you felt as though you were plugged into energy that made you feel alive?

The answer to these questions will help you discover the authentic dream. When you discover your dream within, it sets the intention energy to create it. You won't see anything as a sacrifice, it will create synchronicity, and it will draw the path for you.

Destiny: The biggest question most of us ask is "what is my purpose". Is there a reason I am here? Where am I supposed to be going? Desires motivate us. Dreams create the path. Destiny is walking the path towards where you are to go. Every step, whether we perceive it as positive or negative, carries us towards our destiny. How fast we get there is determined by how much we struggle and fight the path. The reaction we have to any event is what creates the obstacles.

DESTINY JOURNEY

Determining your destiny next line in case anyone is still confused about the difference between journey and visualization I want to touch on those for a moment. A journey is when we step outside of this reality. A visualization is when we are in this reality visualizing what might be or could be. Determining your destiny journey is sort of a combination of a journey and visualization. We want to step out of our reality and go to our temple, our spirits will temple within. So it is party a journey and partly visualization. So what we are going to visualize is this a reality of what could happen. So while we are journeying out of this reality, your visualization will be in this reality. We're also going to do some energetic work. This is how I was taught to see the big picture in a way that I could go back afterwards and really dissect the picture in this reality in order to gain the most wisdom from the pictures shown.

So let's begin by taking a deep breath in through the nose and slowly exhale out through the mouth. And again in through the nose and out through the mouth. Breathe and exhale with a sigh. As you breathe feel your whole body began to relax. Inhale. Exhale. And imagine as you inhale that your lungs are filling up fully and completely. And as you exhale everything is released. As you breathe in and out we feel each new breath revitalize us. With each exhale all the worries and distractions of the day are released and simply slip away. Your stomach expands fully as each breath goes deeper and deeper. Exhale fully once more releasing all that is within.

Now I want see your inner temple begin to appear before you just through the mist. It is familiar. It is familiar because we have visited here many, many times. Yet, today something seems different. And as we slowly begin to approach walking through the mists, we notice that our normal entrance is just behind the mist but a new entrance is awaiting us. We have not noticed this entrance before. This entrance is made from translucent, violet lights. As you approach this entrance, pause taking a deep breath; inhaling the energy that emanates from this entrance.

There is something very different about this entrance, really about this journey. A sacred, holy energy seems to rise from beneath our feet. As we approach the entrance, it is as if the air you breathe whispers a soft melody. A melody of your destiny. As we stepped through the entrance, the luminescence emanates from the walls, the floor, and the ceiling, filling our entire being with a warm safe energy. The marble beneath your feet is cool upon your soles; it fills you with a knowing. Moving slowly torched the center of the room; a violet flame arises from the floor. It is the violet flame of trust. A knowing, and experience within, ensures you that all that occurs in this journey can be trusted. Take a deep breath and allow this flame of trusts to fill you. Allow it to draw you in.

You see a pillow very near the flame. Slowly moving to the pillow you lower yourself to sit down, feeling very relaxed and comfortable as though you had been here many times before. This is your power spot. This is your sacred space to visit your dreams and destinies. To see the big pictures. To connect with your desires. Focus your attention now on the violet flame. Gaze into it. Move your left hand to your heart center. That place between your heart and your throat - right between your breasts. Feel the violet flame penetrate this center giving you a sense of warmth and calmness.

If at this moment you are experience any restless or anxious feelings, take a deep breath. Hold it for a count of three and release it as you exhale all of that restlessness and anxiety. Do this until your entire body feels calm and relaxed. Ask yourself do you have at this moment any disappointments, any hurts, any resentments, or betrayals surrounding your dreams that you are holding on to. Breathe in and out. Simply allow these feelings, these emotions to reveal themselves. Don't try to change them. Just allow them to be. Let them exist and speak to you as they are talking to the person that they are connected to. As you feel in touch with these feelings of disappointment, and hurt, and sadness, and resentment, of lost dreams take a deep breath and hold those feelings. Allow your heartbeat to count for you three beats. Now blow them outward. Release them to the violet flame of trust. Blow them out completely. Give them all to the flame. Again ask yourself these questions, allow them to come up. Is there anything else left? Gift yourself the time to continue this process until you no longer have anything arising from the questions.

Now take another deep breath and exhale feeling lighter. Again and as you breathe in, your hand still on your heart center, imagine and feel and breathe in this violet ray of light. Allow it to penetrate as you breathe it in. Feel it deep within you - filling you. Now repeat to yourself "I have no limitations to fulfilling my longings, my desires, and my dreams. What are my dreams now? What is my soul desire? Listen to what comes up. Watch the pictures being drawn. Allow them to occur. Allow them to be expressed.

Now place your right hand on your heart center, over your left, and breathe this dream you just saw in. Inhale deeply the pictures drawn deep into your heart center. Now at this moment, think of someone you love. Your child, your beloved, your pet, opens your mind to this love and receives it without condition. Allow it to seal this dream. Seal this desire. As you freed your imagination, freed your experience, freed your creative soul, allow the answers revealed to you through the violet flame of trust to be remembered. To be felt. To be experienced in the here and now.

When you are ready to return to this reality, holding this picture sealed deep within your heart center, rise from your power center. Pausing at the Violet Flame of trust speak words of your gratitude for gifting the pictures, gifting the feelings, and gifting the experience. As you exit your inner temple through the door you now know exists, you know it can be returned to at any time to receive more clarity on your dream; you walk barefoot on Mother Earth until you return to the here and now. Simply flex your wrist, flex your ankles to return fully feeling energized and deeply loved.

SOUL PURPOSE SACRED CONTRACT

I (add name), having fearlessly walked the Inner Spoke of the South and discovered my soul purpose, I now make a sacred contract with the Universal Consciousness, the Great Spirit of All.

In the presence of All My Relations, I firmly commit to the following Act of Power: My Soul Purpose is:

_____

_____

I will take the following actions during the next year to walk the sacred path towards my soul purpose:
a.
b.
c.
d.
e.
f.

I give myself permission to grow through each step in the living of my vision. Should I fail to honor my own commitment to this Act of Power, I agree to the giveaway of:_____
Sign and Date

Chapter 25

INNER SPOKE – SOUTHWEST

DIVINE POWER

Virtue: Humility

Intent: To contemplate internal belief
               system and uncover hidden
               emotion

The walk of the fourth inner spoke is like a
gateway to the center of the wheel. It determines
our strength both physically and spiritually. It is
the spoke of pure love. It is the spoke we
challenge our truths of what our emotional
responses are to both the external world and the
inner life. It is a connection to Divine
Power. Yet, it is also the spoke that looks out our
fears of loneliness, following our truth, and of
commitment.

It can be a most difficult spoke to be honest even
with ourselves as we explore the path of the
spoke. In truth, it means that one must love
oneself as the only Path to the Divine. If you
cannot love yourself, then it is very difficult to
allow the unconditional, pure love of the
Divine. It is, at its core, about awakening the
conscious self to be aware of the higher self. It is

about looking at the wounds of the past, finding the pure love and healing those wounds through forgiveness. This is a tall order. The path to spiritual consciousness is the walk of this spoke. Love is Divine Power.

There is an aspect to this spoke which requires commitment. Commitment in its essence is having the willingness to extend love to the furthest stretches possible to give it life. Then taking it further to give it arms and legs to cross the mountains on the journey. This is commitment.

Forgiveness: It is vital to remember that even when you act of anger, regardless of the cause or justification, you are inviting and co creating anger, disharmony, and discord. To find peace, one must become peaceful by seeking to act out of love. This is most difficult when the obstacles are as solid granite and seemingly unjustified. It is only by making the commitment to act out of love that the peace will emerge. Many times the voices behind the anger and resentment that you hear are fueled by another's own fear. An act of love is to hold them in sacred thought asking that they feel safe and loved. Anger may make its point, violence may make a change, but it is only for a moment. After the moment, what I left in its wake is entrails of mistrust which is difficult to erase.

All of this brings us to the most difficult challenge in life – forgiving. Forgiving the ones that you love is much easier than forgiving those whom you feel no love for. At times, it is even more difficult to forgive yourself, but this is a vital necessity in the expansion of your soul. There is a vast difference between having the patience to wait and apathy. Patient waiting is a way of establishing a foundation of trust and faith in the Divine, in the Sacredness of life. Apathy is using doing nothing as an excuse for doing nothing.

Regarding the fear of letting go, stop living in the fear of letting go of what was. You make the choice. Every choice, even the choice to let go, is creating a new reality, a new experience. Embrace it. Yes there maybe sadness and grief in letting go, but replace that with the joy and excitement for what you now have room for. For everything that you let go will be replaced by a gift from the Divine Universe.

Remember too, the act of letting go rather than fighting, this act of surrendering to the Divine Universe is an act of love.

Questions for Journal Entry – Inner Spoke – Southwest

- What wounds do I see on the surface that still needs to be healed? What emotional memories can cause me pain? Anger? Resentment? Jealousy?

Looking at the relationships in my life – both current and past for wounds. Writing names and sitting with the name to see what may come up with each name and writing it out.

- Do I have wounds that I use to control or manipulate others to feel sorry for me? Do I allow others to control me because of their wounds? Because of guilt, shame, or remorse of my own wounds? What can I do to shift my reaction?

- Am I in fear of losing my identity if I heal emotionally? Do I use my emotional health as an excuse not to have an intimate relationship? Can I define myself without speaking or referring to wounds? Am I attached to a negative emotion as a crutch to ease pain?

- Do I understand what forgiveness is really? Can I write my own definition? Can I forgive myself? Can I forgive others for the wounds that they have caused? Can I forgive myself for wounding another? Who can I not forgive? Why? What prevents me from letting go of the wounds?

- What have I done in the past six months that needs to be forgiven? Is there still old wounds that I have not made amends for? Why have I not made amends and forgiven the person and myself? What is being affected by holding onto the situation and pain associated with it? What is the underlying fear?

- Can I define my ideal relationship yet? Do I have a different definition for intimate relationships? For an intimate relationship with self? With the Divine? Do I have a different definition for each friend / coworker / associate / gender? Are my relationships based upon the stories of my wounds? Can I let go of the stories?

All of these questions are difficult to even ask self, let alone answer them honestly. Many times in walking this spoke you can feel the emotional pain of a situation all over again. Again, I remind you that this is not a beat up on you process. The process is designed to uncover, discover, and discard that which is no longer serving my journey. It is simply to see where you are at the moment – to take an inventory. Many times in this process we discover that the real person we need to forgive is ourselves

FORGIVING IS LOVING

Spend time reflecting upon what the word forgiveness means to you. In 4-6 sentences write out your definition of forgiveness.

Go back to your journal work and see who you identified that you still need to forgive. Remember to include those names that you identified fear, resentment, guilt, or other emotion with. AND don't forget to include yourself. Taking the list write a letter to each name expressing all the emotion that is still attached to them. Ceremonially burn the letter. Continue this process of writing letters and burning them to each person until your heart description above matches the words of the letter.
At this point, ask yourself "do I need to make amends to this person?" Only you can answer and determine the amends.

ReWrite The Story

Changing the story. Write 4-6 sentences of who you are at this stage of the journey. Draw line down the page and write 4-6 sentences without using any victim role words of who you want to be. Now look at your sentences and compare with who you want to be with who you are identifying any internal beliefs that need to be adjusted and rewritten.

I Deserve To Receive

Belief that you deserve to receive is one root that must be firmly planted. Whether speaking of receiving the spiritual gift of forgiveness or Divine Love or of the physical manifestation of receiving your dreams, knowing that you have a value in the world is paramount. When we do not feel worthy, we are really saying no to Divine Love. We tend not to appreciate the depth of value of our own unique gifts and confuse value with selfishness.

Rather when you receive your desires and give them value, you are able to give to others with the knowing that all needs of all people are equal in importance. It all starts with the belief that you deserve to receive.

Get barefoot, if you can go outside and stand against Mother Earth all the better.

Take a deep breath in and slowly exhale. Again. Again.

Now imagine your toes are roots growing down deep into the Earth. Those roots tap into a deep, crystal clear pool of water. Savor the sweet nectar of Mother Earth. Allow it to flow up through your roots (toes). Let it fill every cell quenching all thirst.

Open your arms and state out loud as this nectar fills you

"I deserve to receive _____(fill in the blank with your big dream)____"

Keep your hands outstretched as though waiting to receive a warm embrace.

Again with emotion state out loud

"I deserve to receive _____(fill in the blank with your big dream)____ "

Notice how you feel. Notice are speaking timid or boldly?

Again with a bold loud voice:

"I deserve to receive _____(fill in the blank with your big dream)____ "

Practice this each morning for a few weeks and see how you embody the attitude of deserving to receive Divine Love.

FORGIVENESS SACRED CONTRACT

I (add name), having fearlessly walked the Inner Spoke of the Southwest and examined my internal belief system, I now make a sacred contract with the Universal Consciousness, the Great Spirit of All.

In the presence of All My Relations, I firmly commit to the following Act of Power:

I will forgive myself and others in order to receive and accept Divine Love by no longer being a victim. I will do this by adjusting my beliefs, writing forgiveness letters, making amends, and practicing "I deserve to receive" daily. I will complete my forgiveness letters by_____.

I give myself permission to grow through each step in the living of my vision. Should I fail to honor my own commitment to this Act of Power, I agree to the giveaway of:_____
Sign and Date

CHAPTER 26

INNER SPOKE – WEST

WILL POWER

Virtue: Surrender

Intent: What is my purpose?

The challenge of the fourth spoke behind us, we look to the fifth spoke. This spoke is about will power and communication of your power. This spoke looks at how you communicate with others and with yourself. It challenges a surrender of your own will power to that of the Divine. The proverbial "Walk Your Talk". Will power is really nothing more than the power of choice. Be careful here not to sit in judgment but rather look at the choices made in life and reflect upon how they may have resulted differently with different action. Any genuine healing comes from complete honesty with self.

Remember that every choice made, every thought and feeling, are all acts of power. The words spoken are powerful energy. This spoke teaches us that we are responsible for our own power of choice.

- Can you define strong willed? Are you strong willed? Or do other people in your life have control over your will power? Why? Or do you seek out to control others with your will power? Why?

- Are you able to express yourself honestly? Can you do it gently and lovingly? Why Not?

- Can you ask and receive guidance from others? Do you trust guidance from others and the Divine?

- Do you fear Divine guidance? Why?

- What situations cause you to give your will power away?

- Do you try and make bargains with the Divine over the decisions you make? Or do you take responsibility for your choices?

The lesson here is to make no judgments nor have any expectations regarding the choices. Give up on the idea that you need to know exactly why things happen the way they do. Trust that every unscheduled event in life is a form of spiritual direction given to you. Have the courage to make the choices in your own life and accept the responsibility of those choices.

- Do you see it as the power of choice or fate? Do you have the will power to make the choices of your soul or do you return to the logical choices of society? What defines your will power?

Sacred Surrender

The essence of this spoke is surrendering our personal will to Divine will. Allow our opposing perceptions to be composted so that we can open to the perceptions of our soul purpose to the Divine. This means that we must look to the shadows. May times our opposing perceptions are being brought forth from the Saboteur of our own being. This means releasing even more of what we think, what we believe to be truth, and judgment.

Where does will power come in? We have the power of choice that is our will power. The energy we hold in making choices is our will power. Having a strong will power simply means we activate our power of choice by surrendering to the choice of the Creator. Sounds paradoxical,

but is really about balance. Thus the first Power Act is to release to the compost
What you will need for this ceremony:

A piece of cloth
An offering – tobacco, sage, lavender – just a pinch of whatever sacred herb is calling to you
Piece of paper
String to tie the cloth into a bundle

After gathering your items, spend some time in reviewing your answers to see what is needed to be released. What is self-will verse Divine will in your thoughts and actions? What are you doing to sabotage yourself? What seduces you? Write one thing that is the biggest need to release on the paper. Sign it and date it.

Open sacred space as you will.

Place the paper in the center of the bundle and add the offering. Tie it up with the string into a bundle.

When the time is right for a fire, burn the bundle. Now remember that you are paving the way for a clearer and stronger will based in the Divine. When you burn the bundle be sure to speak your intentions aloud to the Creator.
Once the bundle is burned, remove the ashes and bury them to be composted. Again, intention is

everything. By this point you are all well versed in creating your own ceremonies and sacred spaces. Each step is ceremony. Treat it as such and the energy of your intentions will be felt.

Here are some possibilities for statements in this ceremony:

Shift my fear into courage
Release dis-empowerment into confident action
Release shortsightedness into Eagle vision

These are a couple of simple statements that I have used in this ceremony as a sample of the power of words. Remember, it is your intention and words to begin to "walk your talk" that is being engaged.

Song Ritual

Nearly every spiritual path has song, has chant as part of its practice. But what is the real value of song? What does song have to do with surrender? Will power? Divine Power?

As I was taught and experienced once more this morning, the energy centers of the body were explained to me as this by one teacher. We have the root. The base. The foundation. This is our connection to Earth where all our beliefs begin and are deeply rooted within. There is no truer representation of the personal will. All will is based upon our beliefs. We will stand and fight for what we believe in - whether it is in alignment or not. We have a fight or flight response in life that is here, he explained. That if we do not have the roots to fight for - then we take flight.

He goes on to explain, as he experiences it, that the crown is Divine power. It is where all power flows in to the human being. We must be open to Divine power in order to receive it. All receive it, whether it goes anywhere afterwards is dependent upon the connection between the crown and the root. How much caca is in between? What our beliefs are rooted in? Where is our heart? What is our voice speaking? Where our thoughts? Is our mind closed? How about our sexual balance? Our feminine vs masculine energy balance?

According to his experience the five energy centers in between become blocked, obstructed, in active, closed, and wounded which prevents the Divine Power from reaching the root. When this happens surrender is impossible and a person can become lost in Self will power verse being a part of Divine Power.

He would have be sing the vowels. A E I O U. Each vowel sound until it no longer was a chore to sing. Just as the little death breathing exercise it was a practice of holding each sound at a consistent level. And he would push until all five could be sung consecutively without breath.

When this was achieved - to be honest - I thought I had arrived. Yet it goes on. He shared how that was the beginning and proceeded to for a full ninety seconds sing 7 sets of A E I O U without a breath in between. From there he was in a near trance state. He said one can step between the worlds within a breath and back again if they were truly connected and a part of Divine power without obstacle. This, to him, was being a hollow bone which very few ever achieved but we all strives to become closer. This morning I was struck as I went to bury my ashes from my releasing ceremony in a compost pile to bury my feet up to my waist in the warm, smelly compost dirt along with those ashes and begin to sing. When we are surrendering our own will power, it is imperative that we remember we are surrendering power. We are really clearing away all of those ego based, belief based, rooted beliefs that no longer serve us and serve only to block us from the Divine power available. So the sacred act of power here is really a song. A song to your soul.

Begin by simply singing the sound of each vowel - do not worry about the breaths

aaaaaaaaaa, ahhhhhhhhhh, aaaaaaaaa
eeeeeeee,eeeeeeeee,eeeeeeee
iiiiiiiii, iiiiiiiii, iiiiiiiii
ooooooo,ohhhhhhh,ooooooo
uuuuuuuuuuuuuuuuuu

Change the octave, change the tone, and change the level that you sing/chant them. When you are comfortable with each of the sounds, using your own pulse as a timer or watch a clock, sing/chant each vowel by itself for a minute each. Take as many breathes as you need. You are not concerned with that at all at this point. As you continue this practice over the next month, begin to add a and e together for a two minute chant song until you are able to for a full five minutes chant song all five of the vowels. This is a cleansing practice. The more often you create this sacred act of cleansing, the more powerful the song/chant experience. When you are ready begin to focus upon something you need release as you do your five minute song chant. One single thing. Focus only on that one item until you "know" you have released it. This morning knowing what I am releasing needs to be composted, I combined the two ceremonies. Anything is possible to create. Remember with each ritual, with each ceremony, with each journey, what I share is a guide. You are your own teacher, ask spirit to guide your teaching and make each your own.

Releasing Sacred Contract

I (add name), having fearlessly walked the Inner Spoke of the West and examined my will power and the use of my will power, I now make a sacred contract with the Universal Consciousness, the Great Spirit of All.

In the presence of All My Relations, I firmly commit to the following Act of Power:

I will surrender my self-will to Divine Will by _____. In order to surrender, I commit to releasing _____ part of my will power to the Divine by _____.

I give myself permission to grow through each step in the living of my vision. Should I fail to honor my own commitment to this Act of Power, I agree to the giveaway of:_____
Sign and Date

It is vital in this sacred contract to understand that it is a difficult process to surrender. Different layers of will power take on different masks. As you contemplate you sacred contract, select a single aspect of self that needs to be released to work towards surrender. Do not simply state I will surrender.

Remember too that you, to this point have made twelve sacred contracts in a relatively short period of time. The contracts as we move into the Center

Hub become increasingly more in-depth. So break each a part into small pieces so that you can strive towards.

CHAPTER 27

INNER SPOKE – NORTHWEST

POWER OF REASONING

Virtue: Wisdom

Intent: Equality

The sixth spoke is about the power of your thoughts; your mental and reasoning abilities on your beliefs and attitudes in life. It challenges you to have an open mind, receive internal messages both consciously and unconsciously, and to act upon that direction.

It is a wisdom spoke. Wisdom is simply what is accumulated through life experience – that knowledge gained and then applied. The Northwest is our teacher, our educator – the one within and the one outside of physical life.

This spoke teaches us that with our mind we can command energy to become matter. A bridge to the Divine. It is about how we handle change within our mind. The true essence of this spoke is that no one can determine your life path. You do. You make the choice of whether to live in the conscious state or remain 'asleep'. The goal of this spoke is the ability to handle any and all changes in life without fear and simply trust the moment has a message of truth. It is our job to discover that message.

Becoming conscious is being able to change the rules by which you live by and the beliefs you have to a path that is for your highest good.

To this point we have determined a path, made a choice to walk the path even if we did not know where it was going. We took the step. We have looked at letting go of all the things within us that hold us back, we have looked at those weakness; yet, we have also examined many of our strengths, those things which we are exception at. We have looked at where we are bitter and cynical in life to transcend them and transform them into sweet nectar. It is now that we begin to look towards the wisdom gained to transcend it into wisdom to fulfill our dreams and visions. We are standing to prepare ourselves to go beyond what we saw as possible to step into the impossible.

It is always interesting to me that things occur in my own life at the very moment I work upon the spoke to teach. Synchronistic ally this is the spoke of the teacher. I have shared with many of you, I do not teach students, I teach teachers. We are all teachers, but to teach we must gain the wisdom to pass on to others. It is through these beliefs and the shifting of these beliefs that we push from knowledge to wisdom.

Many of our questions overlap from spoke to spoke; keep taking them deeper and deeper down the spiral. Imagine at the moment that you can be, do and experience anything, what will it be? When we reach the end of the inner spokes, we step into recovering our soul. We need know what we are searching for to find it. So as you answer the questions in your journal, as you delve deeper into your beliefs, become vulnerable in your answers. Really allow your truth to take you to the darkest caverns to see what is lying in bones awaiting you.

Questions for Journal Entry – Inner Spoke - Northwest

- Ask yourself what beliefs that you hold onto that cause you to interpret negatively? What beliefs no longer serve you? Why can't you let them go?
- What behaviors do you consistently act upon that cause others to react towards you in a non-desirable way?

- What attitudes do you consistently have that cause you to give away your own power?

- What beliefs do you have that you refuse to let go of that you know are not really truth?

- Where are you judgmental in life? What excuses do you use to justify judging both yourself and others?

- Does change scare you? Why? Is it all change? Or only change that affects your beliefs?

YOUR BELIEFS

Take a few minutes and define your beliefs. List out your top ten foundation beliefs.
1.
2.
3.
4.
5.
6.
7.
8.
9.
10.

After defining them, what beliefs would you like to change and why? Are there any steps that you can take to change them? Write out the steps to change at least one of the beliefs you wish to

222

shift.

VISION STATEMENT

Make a commitment to yourself to write a vision statement for yourself. How do you see you? Is it the same as others see? Do you see the vision for your life? Do you like the picture you are seeing? Is it simply destiny that you call your vision or is there something more?

Many times people have said to me "Carla, your vision is idealistic but unrealistic". Do you listen and adjust your vision because of what others say or feel about it? Is your vision bigger than you can imagine fulfilling? Does that frighten you? Do you tame it down so it will not be so big? Why?

VISION STATEMENT OF PURPOSE SACRED CONTRACT

> I (add name), having fearlessly walked the Inner Spoke of the Northwest and discovered my personal vision statement, I now make a sacred contract with the Universal Consciousness, the Great Spirit of All.
>
> In the presence of All My Relations, I firmly commit to the following Act of Power: My Vision Statement is:

I will take the following actions during the next year to walk the sacred path towards my Vision:

❖ a.

❖ b.

❖ c.

❖ d.

❖ e.

❖ f.

I will take the release the following beliefs during the next year to walk the sacred path towards my Vision:

❖ a.

❖ b.

❖ c.

❖ d.

I give myself permission to grow through each step in the living of my vision. Should I fail to honor my own commitment to this Act of Power, I agree to the giveaway of:_____

Sign and Date

CHAPTER 28

INNER SPOKE – NORTH

GATEWAY TO DIVINE

Virtue: Discernment

Intent: Where I come from

The connection with Divine is an opening or a
gateway to the Cosmic Universe. What can be
discovered about self in stepping through the
gateway? The Universe has the ability to
transcend the limits that our earthly teachers and
even our spiritual guides have. It can challenge
our own abilities, thoughts, beliefs, and
connection. When we stand at the gateway open
to receive, the path way that was once believed to
be narrow, widens into a vastness of infinity that
the human soul can only experience, yet never
fully describe.

This connection can be a profound and
transforming quest into the power that lies outside
of self and yet resides within. The gateway holds
the vessel of wisdom to sip from, not gulp. It is
vital to undertake it with no expectation or

judgments. It will question your personal belief structure and give root to a new foundation to stand in a changing world.

This spoke can define your beliefs and attitudes towards the spiritual world, a journey that can reveal whether your spirit is scattered from the places of your unfinished business to responsibilities and bringing them back into complete unity. The very essence of this spoke is to live in the present moment in unity with the Divine. This is not a spoke that is simply walked upon and left. It is continuous; though you may return to walk another spoke on another journey, all spokes will return to here through the center of the wheel. It is here that you find your life purpose.

In order to find one's authentic life purposes it is vital to ensure that the fears, wounds, and judgments have been healed to a healthy state. Reunification of the spirit into a whole being, ensuring all fragments have been weaved back together.

Questions for Journal Entry – Inner Spoke – North

- Do you know your life purpose? Do you have a fear with truly knowing your purpose? Can you begin to define the Divine?

- Do you judge your life in your journey to discover and come to trust the Divine? Do you question your own faith? Do you feel at times that you have failed the Divine in the choices you have made? Or do you see them simply as lessons?

- Do you have a spiritual path you are following? Why or why not?

- Do you complain about your life to the Divine? Or are you giving gratitude?

- Do you believe it is possible to communicate directly with the Great Spiritual Universe?

- Can you hear and understand the whispers of the winds? How else does the Divine translate wisdom to you? How does when begin to translate the spiritual vibrations from the Universe?

- Does the power of the Universal connection exist within you? Or outside of you?

- How often do you reach out to the Divine spirit to develop the connection? What methods do you feel most connected to the Universe?

- Do you have a spiritual teacher/elder/guide (either in the physical or in the spiritual world) that gives direction to your journey? Do you need one? Is it a necessity for growth? Who or what do you turn to go deeper and enhance the spiritual experience? What do you gift in return for the guidance given?

- Is there a difference between a spiritual experience and a spiritual awakening? Can you define each?

- Are there blocks or obstacles standing in the way of the gateway? Is it within you? With the deeper soul self?

- Are you ready for the knowing that comes with the gateway to the Universe? Do you fear the changes this may bring into your life? What challenges may face you as you step through the gateway? Are you willing to let go of life to learn new lessons?

- Are you willing to do the work that comes with intense spiritual growth?

While this is only a beginning, the spoke is a lifetime of gateway; a lifetime of going deeper into void of mystery. At each gateway, the questions must be asked again and again in a deeper personal self-inventory.

WHAT IS DISCERNMENT?

What is discernment? Easy definition – your bullshit detector. Everything is a truth for someone, everything is false for someone – your truth is found through the art of silent witness. You learn by observing all, then interpret what you observe based upon your life experience, and then you determine (discern) what is your truth.

Silent Witness or the art of observation is really understanding the mirror. The energetic world is really a mirror to within. There are four parts to discernment as I was taught.

1. Observing the shadows – We are looking for the cause of the shadow. What in your life is causing tension be it in the physical, mental, emotional or spiritual aspects of life? Remember the question "where can you be seduced?"

2. Cultivating Silence – We are looking here for the symbols, the medicine, or the message found in the shadows. Our mindlessness process, our cultivation of being silent and non-attachment, allows us to stretch to open mind without our

preconceived experiences entering the symbols, medicine or messages.

3. Translating our spiritual Language – We are looking here for what our symbols mean, what the medicine means, and what the messages mean. Remember that we all translate differently so it is vital to have developed this process when looking at discernment. One of the first set of symbols that we must develop here is what your symbol for yes and no is.

4. Experiencing the Pulsation – We are looking for the variation in pulses of the vibrations. The clarity comes from the emotional being here; yet, we remain detached for the emotion. A paradox.

STEPPING INTO THE SILENCE OF DISCERNMENT

A. Starting at your feet, place your full concentration downward relaxing them until they are completely relaxed. Now give yourself the intention that no more signals shall be received from the feet for any movement.

B. Repeat this for each section of the body going upwards. I.e. the legs, the pelvic area, the stomach area, the back, the shoulders, the fingers, the arms. Take your time here and make sure to give yourself the intention.

C. When you reach the brow, rather than focusing downward, shift to upward.

D. Hold the sense of focusing upward from the brow for three heartbeats before setting the intention of dropping down.

E. Count backwards from 10 to 1knowing at 1 you will be in the center of silence within

F. Within this silence ask your questions, receive the gifts, and reclaim any power that is held here to bring back with you.

G. When you ready, simply count upwards to 10 taking deep cleansing breaths.

H. Be sure to give yourself time to relax before getting up.

STANDING AT THE GATEWAY

This is a huge spoke that is a connection to all things in the Upper Worlds.

Standing at the Gateway to the Divine, we must prepare ourselves for the journey ahead. The Divine worlds (the Upper Worlds) journey has been called the hero's journey. It is where, in the realms of spirit, that one can learn the true nature of their purpose – every contract or agreement your soul has made can be revealed in this journey. There is a caveat. The hero's journey is one of climbing to the highest peaks of the mountains. In the spirit realms this requires that one be cleansed or purified of self.

Purifying of self is really much of what the walk of the inner spokes has prepared you for. You have seen your beliefs – those that limit you especially or seduce you. It is here that we step in the sacred silence to purify ourselves in order to move into the spirit realms of the Upper Worlds. This cleansing or purifying allows for the reunification process to happen on all levels of the Upper World. Some of the most difficult beliefs held are often confused with reality. Security can cause us to use beliefs around time, money or courage to maintain our hold tightly. We cling to the limiting believe rather than risk exploring what life would be if we released it. This idea of security has held many in a limiting belief that they are still students – they are not ready to step fully into their own power and their destiny. So we avoid it, side step it, and challenge it.

In this exercise we are going to review our journals of the spokes done thus far to find our answers. Be as honest as possible.

When I _____ then I will be able to _____.

Begin with your relationships - Your love relationships, your family relationships, and your work relationships.

When I discover _____ love relationship, then I will be _____
Example: When I discover the right love relationship, then I will be fulfilled in life.

Move into your emotions

When I learn how to _____ I will be able to
_____
Example: When I learn how to let go of my resentment, then I will be able to forgive.

You can take this into every area of your life from your career to your health. The first blank you fill in for each area is your limiting belief that must be cleansed/purified from your life. Look for patterns or the same words being used in either the first blank or the second blank. While it may seem too simplistic of an exercise, it is in the simplicity that the revealing happens.

When you have discovered the limits that you are still binding yourself with, you can use any of these releasing rituals to begin the process of cleansing and purifying the spirit.

Fire ceremony is a beautiful way to connect with the light energies and release the energies within

233

that are binding us. Just as we make the choice to release the need to grasp tightly, draw lines, and incite a fear personally, we must release this same energy in the world. We must release prejudgment, competitive natures, lack of respect and honor for the lands we walk upon, and the fear of lack. We must release so that can restore balance in the world to allow for a new kind of fire - a fire full of Eternal Flames of Love within its energy. A simple fire ceremony:

Everything is ceremony and sacred even as you create your fire itself. Speak words of gratitude for all that is being gifted. Bring an offering to the fire – something from nature like a flower or a pinecone. Blow into the offering whatever it is that you want to release or heal in your life to make room for the new. When you offer it to the fire, say a prayer of gratitude. It is a symbolic release and a symbolic claiming of the new energy.

Every spoken word is an act of creation. An act that sends ripples of energetic signatures into the world. Stand with your feet upon Mother Earth, lift your arms to welcome the energies, and speak your words of intention, speak your words of intention to release what no longer serves you, and speak your words of intention of gratitude for what has received.

Walking meditation, during this meditation you focus on the right placement of your feet as you walk. Walk slowly, yet confidently, carefully placing your feet on the ground, as you walk forward.

The awareness of the various parts of your feet as they touch the ground, give you the encouragement that you are walking steadily. That you are connecting with the ground beneath your feet. Place one foot in front of the other with grace an awareness. Walk in this way in silence, breathing deeply in a comfortable relaxed rhythm. Walk for 15 minutes. Early morning is the best time to do this mediation. Choose a place in nature if possible, where you will not be disturbed. If you are walking indoors walk in a big circle.

With each step you take speak your intention of releasing a single limit. Keep it very simple as you work the meditative journey. Don't try to do multiple intentions at once.

REUNIFICATION

Whenever a person suffers any type of trauma (or even euphoria – the feeling can never recapture the euphoric experience again), they may have a profound experience of feeling as though something is missing within or that they have lost something; an experience of dissociation with life. This is really about a part of a person's energy that is no longer accessible to them, whether the inaccessibility is because the essence or energy is within or outside of the physical body.

Reclaiming the "missing" part can be done by "soul retrieval". The basic premise of soul retrieval is either the person suffering the loss or someone on their behalf goes back in time to the experience and reclaims the lost piece bringing it back to the soul. So you are doing journey work, past life regression, and symbolic or metaphoric ceremonial work. All of which is only undertaken after the mending process (hopefully).

In this exercise, we are going to allow each to have the experience of reunification (if there is a fragment missing).

We begin with the understanding that light will be a metaphorical relationship for our soul. This metaphor gives us something to work with to find that which is hidden. You may find a different set of metaphorical symbols that work for you. In my experience, many times we see energy in the form of light – different colors representing different portions of energy. It is imperative to remember in this exercise, we are not looking at anything but our own energy. Everything that is done has ripple effects – so caution is warranted.

Begin by determining the time frame of the loss that you wish to reclaim (never work with more than a single event).

Next, determine what exactly is missing from the event. Example: is it a belief that no longer has purpose? Or is it an identity issue – meaning cannot experience who wishes to be? Or is it connectedness – meaning love lost as example?

Now find a symbolic image of what is missing. Can you go back to a time when this image was part of you?

Now you will want to open your sacred space, speak to your gatekeeper and state your intention of a desire to go back to the time when you lost the symbolic image before proceeding. Pause before doing that and read the rest of the exercise.

Once you are in your sacred space, received an affirmative response from your gatekeeper to continue on this reunification process, begin to visualize a mirror in front of you. A two-way mirror that stretches above your head and below your feet. The mirror at the moment is foggy, images are not clear. Reach your hand towards the mirror and touch it. As you touch it the fog dissipates and you see yourself in reflection.

Remove your hand and watch as the mirror becomes foggy again. Inhale deeply three times.

State your intention to see the moment in time when you "lost" the piece you are retrieving and then reach out to touch the mirror again. Freeze the image and watch frame by frame to see the moment when the "loss" occurred. Remember, it is here you may see the symbolic image you set before or you may see the loss as light. When you discover the moment that your essence was lost, ask the question "Can I return this fragment to essence in the now?" Listen for the answer. If you receive a yes, continue. If you receive the answer of no, heed the answer and leave the mirror for another time. It is far better to prepare the now to receive the energy then to bring it back too soon and cause further energetic disruption.

When you receive the answer yes, push your hand through the mirror and take the image or the light into your hand. Many times you will see the energy move up your arm of its own accord. Remember you are reunifying the energy – you are not becoming the symbol or the energy. There may also be times when as you attempt to touch the energy that it will dissipate like sand in the wind. If this happens, imagine your palm is like a magnet that draws the energy in it.

Once you have the energetic symbol or essence, withdraw your hand from the mirror and place your palm in between your heart and throat area feeling the energy integrate within.

Touch your hand on the mirror again to see your energy body reflected back at you. See the energy begin to weave itself back together. When the reunification is complete withdraw your hand from the surface of the mirror.

Be sure to thank your guide/gatekeeper who watched your essence while you worked and close your sacred space.

As a side note to this exercise, I actual have a small mirror that I use specifically to see the energy body of self. It is dark colored mirror (much like a scyring mirror) that I now use for this purpose rather than visualizing the mirror. I also use an obsidian egg at times as the mirror reflection. Find what works for you. The imperative piece is that you work with one aspect at a time and that you have done the work before attempting to bring the energy back into self.

DISCERNMENT SACRED CONTRACT

I (add name), having fearlessly walked the Inner Spoke of the North and discerned my soul purpose, I now make a sacred contract with the Universal Consciousness, the Great Spirit of All. In the presence of All My Relations, I firmly commit to the following Act of Power:

I will practice discernment in all aspects of my journey.

I will take the following actions during the next year to walk the sacred path in discernment:

a.

b.

c.

d.

e.

f.

I give myself permission to grow through each step in the living of my vision. Should I fail to honor my own commitment to this Act of Power, I agree to the giveaway of:_____
Sign and Date

CHAPTER 29

INNER SPOKE – NORTHEAST

WARRIOR SPIRIT

Virtue: Integrity

Intent: Strength

The final spoke of the inner spoke walk is the warrior. The life of the spiritual warrior is a challenging one. The basic choice of a warrior is whether to engage life fully or exist in life. It is the impeccability of a walk that allows for the integration of walking your words.

The life path of anyone who walks within their own truths and attempts to live an impeccable life is in essence living the life of a Warrior spirit. To engage fully means to take responsibility for everything that comes into our lives in order to gain wisdom, but more importantly to find our true selves.

It means that walking the with the warrior spirit you are willing to see from all perspectives including those not of your sight. It means that you are willing to go beyond the obvious aspects of a situation to a deeper than surface life meaning. There is no denial, no acting like a victim; it is making the choice to call the challenges into life not waiting for them. It means becoming aware of the influences of our own past and clearing them fully in order to face new challenges and test with an openness and deeper level of responsibility.

It is then that we become truly receptive to see what you are really confronted with in finding the answer as to why you have called any challenge into your life. It is here that you can learn the best way to work with a challenge and be completely in the flow of the challenge without hesitation.

Whenever you take an action with warrior spirit especially, it reverberates. It is like the proverbial stone thrown into the water. Once the stone is thrown into the air, it cannot be retrieved or changed. The action is done. When the stone hits the water it will cause ripples and each ripple has an effect upon the vibration of everything surrounding it. The ripples go beyond the scope of human sight.

The shadow of the spoke is the rescuer which assists and then withdraws under the illusion of detachment. It is the hero who becomes addicted to the rescue. It is said that this is the most difficult spoke of all the spokes to walk upon. To truly know self, be willing to defend your own ethics with sword, and to walk impeccably are difficult and at times lonely actions.

First, I will share the questions to reflect upon in your journal work. We will then go deep into developing our own code of ethics, the responsibility of walking as a warrior without premature deduction, and how we walk our talk.

The Warrior

To be actively engaged energetically in an experience whether it is with a universal enemy, your own self-ignorance or with the ultimate flow of cosmic energy is a journey for self -discovery.

That journey is taken to benefit self and others not to focus on a single individual, but rather the complete and right practice of balance.

To have the ability to see with the heart as a truth – an absolute essential ability – not see what is perceived.

To constructively seek out answers for solutions, not await for them to be brought to you.

Joy, light, sadness, conflict, and the void part of expansiveness is breathed in and accepted.

Death and life is seizing the day for all – one heart beat at a time.

Being committed to letting go and never forcing.

Seeing the conflict and being mindful of suffering and repercussion, the knowing that absences exist within the void.

Observing with calmness and wisdom each heart beat to know reality as it truly is in all inner dimensions.

Knowing all the ripples, the waves, and the undertows, yet stepping into the rapids anyways. This is the way of the warrior.

Questions for Journal Entry – Inner Spoke – Northeast

- Are you willing to follow your own way? The path of the warrior spirit can be a lonely path.

- Are you willing to carry a shield and sword? It is said that the warriors shield is their code, their sword enlightenment, will is their armor, the immovable mind their castle and faith their strength.

- Are you willing to seek out challenges of living? Can you see life as challenges rather than drama 'stories' to be read? Are you willing to work the mind to conquer the warrior within in order to allow the warrior spirit to emerge?

- Can you define your personal code? Enlightenment? Do you believe that disciple can become the new sword of the enlightened mind? What does disciple involve?

- Do you understand that the only actions you can control are that of your own? Do you believe that the one thing that you have that no one can take away from you is your connection to the Divine?

- What is honor defined as for you? Is your honor your word? Can you stand in your truth without being bought, bullied or negotiated with?

- Do you believe that how you respond to challenges determines who you are truly? What are the responses you have made lately? Are those of a warrior? Or a victim?

- Can you define the immovable mind? Can you be completely open and non-judgmental?

Walking between the worlds is challenging. Standing at the warrior's gateway it goes to the depths of integrity and honor. It is a gateway of discipline, loyalty and courage of the heart. The Universal spirit of the warrior is what binds all things together in strength. It allows the flow through us as we flow through it.

CODES OF THE WARRIOR ENERGY

Let us begin this portion of the lesson with looking at a few of the codes of the warrior energy

HONESTY
It is imperative that each be honest with self and with interactions with others. For many it is difficult to understand when life seems to be in shades of black, white, and gray how there is a defined right and wrong within the warrior energy. It comes not from what is truth but rather from what is your truth. What is your code of ethics for your walk.

BEHAVIOR
With every action taken it is done with detachment; meaning that all are respected and treated with respect regardless of another person's words, actions, or intentions. The warrior energy see's things as a sacred witness and takes nothing personally; yet always acts with compassion. Compassion is the service to All.

COURAGE

Courage simply means that the knowing of self-truth overcomes fear. There is no room for fear and when one finds themselves in fear they simply look for the knowing to overcome. It is imperative to understand this does not mean it is blind courage, conversely, it is intelligence coupled with strength.

HONOR

There is only one judge that matters in honor – your own inner judge. Your decisions, how you make those decisions and how you carry out your decisions is a reflection of your honor. Your actions must be done with sincerity. Sincerity does not have to make promises because your honor code is such that you walk your talk. It is a duty to walk your talk taken on by the Warrior energy.

So how does one undertake such imposing codes? Before we go into the act of writing our Code of Ethics, it is prudent to go into a journey and meet YOUR Warrior Mentor. Your Warrior Mentor will provide you with strength and wisdom to carry out the act of creating your code of ethics as well as walking your code of ethics.

To begin open your sacred space with the intent of meeting your Warrior Mentor. Ask your Gatekeeper for assistance in going to the Upper Worlds in order to fulfill your intent.

Allow your breathing to slow into your Little Death Breathing.

Once you are ready and have been granted permission from your Gatekeeper, enter your Inner Temple. You notice that there is a heavy oak door that you had not seen before in all the journeys to your Inner Temple. There is strange carvings on the door that you approach to take a closer examination of.

There is a large brass lock with a key held within it. Turning the key slowly you open the door.

Before you is a path unlike any you have ever seen before.

As you step onto the path lined with ancient living oak trees, you notice between the trunks your power animals are there to protect and guide you on this journey. As you follow the path, you notice your breathing and body begin to shapeshift ever so slightly as you step into your "other self".

Just ahead there is a bridge. A bridge of colored energy. It is beautiful – perhaps even the most beautiful arrangement of living color that you have ever seen. Approaching the bridge you cannot help but reaching out to touch the rails. The purity of the color enters your fingertips. Crystal clear light displays, yet solid to the touch as your step onto the bridge. As you walk across the surges of colored energy flow through your entire being, purifying and regenerating your fibers.

As you reach the other side of the bridge, you notice a bell shaped flower hanging just to the side. It captivates your attention. Wanting to hear the song of its ringing, you simply ask for it to sing. Like a wafting tendril of energy, the song rings out three times before a whisper in the winds ask you what your intention of crossing the bridge are.

Your answer to meet your Warrior Mentor.

The bell shaped flower sings once more before all is silent as the last tendrils sing out. A figure appears from a mist of energy to slowly approach. Every movement tall and full of power, the gait one of strength emanating. Without words they turn and you follow. A small fire awaits with two large rocks shaped perfectly for resting upon. You both take your seats.

The figure asks your intentions. You speak your intentions and wait for a reply. If your Warrior Mentor knows you are ready for this journey, they will spend time sharing knowledge and guidance. Listen well.

When it is time for your departure, you speak to your Warrior Guide thanking them for their wisdom and footsteps before you. When you rise to take leave your Warrior Mentor may have a gift for you or final words, pause for a moment and listen. Return across the colored light bridge knowing you may return now at any time to gather strength, practice the arts of a warrior and partake in further knowledge. Pause to acknowledge your power animals before returning to the large oak door. Thank your Gatekeeper before you leave your Inner Temple.

Be sure to drink plenty of water upon your return to the Middle World as the energy of the bridge may leave you feeling light headed.

Remember this, the warrior's path is like a dance that has no specific steps to learn. The dance cannot be taught. There are some that will dance a rapid and frenzied dance while others will dance a seduction dance. All are perfect for the individual – you cannot compare one to another for they are simply different. Because the steps cannot be taught and can only be experienced, this journey should not be taken lightly. Do not attempt to rush it.

The warrior energy is fluid and must shift harmoniously. The most dangerous aspect of this shifting is falling into the trap of belief. It was shared with me that one must believe in a controlled witness way. Meaning you believe in actions. To simply state you believe in something removes the accountability aspect. The accountability aspect is the examination without attachment – that sacred witness perception. It is making an active choice to engage without knowing – simply believing your truths. In practical terms this means every choice is looked upon, you examine all aspects (follow the energy signature) of a choice, all outcomes (all the ripples), and make a conscious choice.
Our next lesson is on the impeccability aspect of the Warrior energy and beginning to formulate our Code of Ethics.

PERSONAL CODE OF ETHICS

Let's start with what might be in a Personal Code of Ethics

We hear different words relating to ethics, but how do you express it in your code so that it means something? Here are a few examples.

INTEGRITY

I will be honest, especially with myself. I will be forthright. I will be sincere. I will be reliable.

LOVING

I will be loving, especially with myself. I will try to be considerate. I will not intentionally hurt anyone, including myself.

COURAGE

I will be courageous in my actions, in spite of fear. I will stand up for my truths.

So now you have the idea let us dive into how you will create your personal code of ethics.

Write down 4-5 sentences that would describe you. "Jane Doe is hard-working. Jane Doe treats others with dignity. Jane Doe is compassionate." (example)

Next write down your personal beliefs that you have discovered in your walk around the inner spokes. What characteristics did you discover are really important to you? What is really, really important to you? What is it that you desire to be rather than what you are now? (i.e. what are you working towards in beliefs?)

Remember that your code of ethics set the tone for how you live your life and how others

252

perceive you. This does not mean you will never make mistakes or never compromise. What it does mean is when you make a mistake – you own it, take responsibility for it, and apologize with being defensive or blaming.

Your code of ethics should be applicable to your home relations, your community relations, and your business relations. We don't wear different masks in different situations. You either are or you're not!

Once you have your short list of ethics, you can go on to creating your sacred contract with self-using those codes. Personal Code of Ethics

For most, the first power contract ever made is when they write down personal truths in the formal of spiritual ethic codes. This process is difficult and time consuming, but the rewards are new gateways revealed. Developing your own personal code of ethics is truly one of the most important gifts you can give to yourself. This process puts into writing those ideas and beliefs that are the very essence of your life. It allows you to say I will do this because I believe this. Having it in black and white allows you to carry with you a reminder of what you believe and gifts you the encouragement and strength to walk your walk.

If you have taken this journey around the spokes, taken the time to write down your answers and your truths, you have already made a major step in developing your own code of ethics. This is a reflection of who you believe you are. From your journal entry, begin to write down all of the traits that you discovered. Both those you consider strengths and those you consider weakness. One or two words on each trait is all needed.

Now make a list of your ethical beliefs. Do not concern yourself with rationalizing or justifying why you believe something. Just list out your beliefs. These are the beliefs that define your decision-making in day to day life.

Now make a list of your ideal relationship. List at least ten things that you believe are vital to any relationship – not only partnership but all relationships.

Once you have done the above, it is time to write and develop your personal code of ethics. This is for you. Not for the world around you. The first thing you write down is what is the purpose of your writing your own code? To become...... To grow .... To be aware ..... Whatever you're your purpose is, this is philosophy behind your code. The only requirement here is that the purpose and the code be tailored to your specific needs.

The second part of the code is the power contract portion. This is where you set up your "I will's" based upon who you are. Go through the lists that you wrote and look to see what matches up to what you believe. Look at the weakness and write a sentence of what you aspire to have for a trait to develop.

The last part of your code of ethics is a sentence or two as to why this important. Why is it important for you personally to apply your personal code of ethics to your life? Once you are done writing your code of ethics set it aside, spend some time in prayer and meditation asking if you have left anything out that should be included. Refine it as necessary and as changes/growth expands in your life.

CODE OF ETHICS SACRED CONTRACT

I (add name), having fearlessly walked the Inner Spoke of the Northeast and examined my internal belief system, I now make a sacred contract with the Universal Consciousness, the Great Spirit of All.

In the presence of All My Relations, I firmly commit to the following Code of Ethics:

Responsibilities to Self:
1.
2.
3.

(example: 1. I will maintain a healthy body by healthy eating and regular exercise.

2. I will practice self-love by nurturing my spiritual life through daily practice of _____.

3. I will be have integrity by being authentic in truths through words and actions.)

Responsibilities to Family:
1.
2.
3.

Responsibilities to Community:
1.
2.
3.

Responsibilities to my Work:
1.
2.
3.

Responsibilities to Nature:
1.
2.
3.

I give myself permission to grow through each step in the living of my vision. Should I fail to honor my own commitment to this Act of Power, I agree to the giveaway of:_____

Sign and Date

This can be as detailed as you desire or as simple as you wish.   The key is to begin writing them down.

CHAPTER 30

INNER SPOKE CONCLUSION

Approaching the East once more, we find the walk of the Inner Spokes has imprinted itself upon our core essence; perhaps even shaking our inner being as we engaged in the accounting of our souls. We examined and contemplated not only our thoughts and beliefs, but determined which we wish to live by. Pausing at this time to reflect upon the deep spiritual engagement is imperative.

Standing in the Northeast to look towards the East of the wheel, we find ourselves in awe and reverence for all that is, the winds whisper "divine devotion daily".

Divine Devotion Daily is simply taking moments each day to mindfully attend to our spirits. A simply walk in nature, listening to music that touches your soul, or soul diving meditation. Mindfully stepping into sacred space of the soul is vital to create space for Spirit.

Divine Devotion Daily is establishing a spiritual connection to all that is. It engages every part of the human being – our mind, our bodies, our emotions, and our spirits. It is a vital aspect of living in a balanced and harmonious way. It is this daily devotion to the Divine that establishes the deep and profound experiences; giving us life purpose and meaning.

Daily Divine Devotion can be as simple as focusing upon the breath. The breath experience is one tangible expression of being. Every living being takes a breath. It reminds us that we are all connected, we are all interrelated. It allows for the Divine Creator to have space in which to enter our core essence.

As you reflect upon the Inner Spokes and all that they have gifted in teaching their medicine, spend moments inhaling deeply and exhaling fully while giving gratitude to the Divine Creator for your journey thus far.

CHAPTER 31

THE CENTER HUB

As we transition from the Inner Spokes to the Center Hub, we must take a moment to reflect upon the connectedness of the spokes with the center hub.

The East Inner Spoke leads directly to the East on the Center, yet, the Southeast leads to both the South and the East. The Southeast is healing, relationships, and the 4 legged world. Now as we connect to the Center, we must look at the Southeast as it relates to both the East (spring, beginning, tribe, sun, 2 legged) and the South (personal power, winged world, summer, growth). The introduction given to the Inner Spokes is only but a beginning, the spiral of each individual spoke and how it interrelates with other spokes is endless.

Example, if you wish to heal the Warrior spirit within in order to find more personal power, what spokes would you walk upon? And how would you travel the wheel to find your way? What other spokes are walked upon to find your way? To heal (SE) the Warrior (NE) spirit (center) to discover personal power (S) … do you walk through the Inner Spokes, the Center Spokes, or travel the Center Hub?

As we move into the Center Hub it is vital that you have your journals of the earlier walks to refer to. Upon each of the four cardinal directions of the Center Hub we will look at the spiritual accounting of the internal as it relates to the direction.

SPIRITUAL ACCOUNTING

The spiritual accounting comes from your journals. Where did you discover strengths as it relates to the web of life, the human family, the unity of all, and the great family? Where did you discover weaknesses? What are the ideals discovered for each of the cardinal directions? What are your goals in reaching those ideals? What power or soul contracts are you willing to make in relationship to the Center Hub Directions?

CHAPTER 32

CENTER HUB – EAST

WEB OF LIFE

Virtue:	Awareness
Intent:	Awareness of Oneness
Goal:	Oneness
Mantra:	I am one with All

The medicine wheel Center Hub is perhaps the most widely seen symbolic image related to the wheel. It is seen as the four directions. The medicine wheel is a way of making sacred space tangible. From ancient times it has been used to create change and healing within those who walk it. The wheel creates a map of sorts to the sacred landscape we live in. It is always spinning or rotating just as the Earth does. And just as all things in life are, with you deep within the center.

The universal symbol of wholeness is the circle; for it is when we are at the ending of one we always find ourselves at the beginning once more. In this web of life that is the very essence of the medicine wheel, we discover ideas and acquire new meanings to life.

If we look at the web of life in nature, the circle is the most common shape. Everything in nature has some aspect of it that is a circle. There is an old Lakota sage Black Elk that said "Everything the Power of the World does is done in a circle. The sky is round, and I have heard that the earth is round like a ball, and so are all the stars. The wind, in its greatest power, whirls. Birds make their nest in circles, for theirs is the same religion as ours." The cells of our DNA are round. A tree is counted in age by the number of rings in its truck. Water ripples when a stone is thrown in. The web of life interconnects us all. We are all related.

We are taught that we pray for all relations – the outer spokes – as we are all part of this sacred circle of life; this web of life. The symbolism of the wheel is that of reflections in perspective. The world view of the web of life is to see that from all places we are connected with all parts of life. I once had a teacher explain the wheel as a mirror. He said that the universe is truly a mirror of all relations and that I can see the truth of my reflection in the center of the hub.

263

While all agree upon the shape of the medicine wheel, the hub represents core principles and qualities of life while the spokes demonstrate that the points are all interconnected to one another as they all emerge and flow from the center. While all traditions in principle and qualities may agree, the symbolism may shift.

The East is the sun rise, the beginning of spiritual renewal. It teaches us to look upon the web of life with innocence of youth. Each blade of grass, every insect, to every star in the skies are sacred. It is standing in the East that the world emerges from the darkness to be reborn into the dawning of a new day. It is becoming focused upon the now and live fully in the present.

In returning to the web of life, the hub of the East, we return to look upon all the other spokes that we have walked to see with fresh new eyes where our focus has been and where we wish it to be. Return to your journals and look upon your relatedness to all kingdoms and see where you stand in the web of life.

Creating Tribe Awareness

It is vital at this point to have a tribe of 4-6 people whom we work with, support, be supported and hold one another accountable. This allows for the experience of oneness to occur on a smaller level. Regular gatherings of this small tribe can create a container to hold the sacred intent of all other work within.

Find 4-6 other's that you can create a tribe with whether it is face to face or virtual. Commit to one another that you will gather at least four times of the year to reflect upon the sacred direction. Ensure that each person has an accountability partner. This is one other individual whom can support and hold you accountable for your actions on your sacred contracts.

The ancient teachings of the Medicine Wheel all reflect the inherent truth that the wheel is a reflection. The Cosmos or the Universe is a reflection of all the people and each person is a reflection of one another. Basically, you see (perceive) life as a reflection of yourself. If you love life, are optimistic, and content what you will see reflected in the Universe is love, beauty, and peace.

It is here that we take our accounting and make a blue print for the next year; a blue print for life that lays out a manner of living in a sacred manner. This is sacredness to all things, to all our relations, and in a harmonious and peaceful way. Only you, after making your personal walk, can make this contract.

As we prepare for the blue print of life, we must pause and reflect upon the meaning within the Circle of Life, our piece.

Ask yourself:

- What does the symbol of the sacred hoop represent within?
- What does the basic four directions represent?
- What does the elements represent?
- What is the gift of the East?

The Sacred Web of Life is not about focusing upon a figure, an object, or even a teaching; it is our own awareness and responsibility of the whole circle. It is the awareness that all is Sacred in Life, all is related, and all must consciously participate if unity is to be achieved.

Meditation for Humanity

Begin by doing deep breathing in through your nose and fully exhaling through your mouth. Allow the tip of your tongue to touch the roof of your mouth just behind your teeth. Focus on your own capacity for love, inhaling deeply, feel your strength within. Exhaling fully connect your own being with the energetic flow as you become grounded within Mother Earth.

As you inhale, feel the connection as you draw in the energy of love fully. Allow it to fill your being. Feel it flow through your lungs and heart, down through your core and into your toes. Inhale this energy until your feel it pulsating throughout every cell in your body focusing on the inhalation.

As the pulsation fills you, begin to shift your focus to the exhalation. As you continue to inhale the energy of love, see the suffering in humanity. Allow your exhalation to connect with the situation that fills your thoughts. Let the healing energy of love flow to the situation.

Return to feel the inhalation of love pulsating as you breath deeply filling you once more. Again shift your focus to another situation to send energetically the loving and healing energy to

Mother Earth. Continue this breath repetition as long as you wish.

When you are ready inhale deeply allowing the energetic signature of love to course through your veins and your exhale flows down into Mother Earth. Again inhale deeply feeling the pulsation pushing deeper into the Earth connecting you and grounding you.

When we find ourselves saddened by events that happen in the world, allowing ourselves the time to connect and energetical heal through meditation gives us an empathic way to heal ourselves and our world in our own way.

The Sacred Tree of Oneness

The Blueprint of Oneness is an exercise that allows one to create mudras with the hands in order to trigger and engage oneness in any setting. The mudras follow a specific blueprint of cellular design. This can produce a most profound experience.

It is a celebration. It is oneness merging. It is life giving to the web of life. It is harmonious. It is to make aware and to experience awareness of oneness.

You need a tree preferably with roots deep in Mother Earth.

You need three giveaways – Something that represents your intention of oneness, something to represent the outer spoke you stand upon (ex a feather or a shell), and something that represents your nourishment or energy exchange to the Tree (ex cornmeal or tobacco)
Four representations of the four directions placed around the tree placed inside a basket or container
You will need staff but this is a very different type of staff. This is a branch that has fallen to the ground – not something you cut or buy – attach anything of oneness, unity, ancestors meaning to you personally.
Sacred herbs (sage or sweetgrass or copal)

Once you have gathered everything together and placed it out around the representation of the Sacred Tree of Life, begin with opening of your sacred space, calling your ancestors, and offering prayer such as:

Great Spirit, the giver of life, I call to you so that I may honor you within this circle of life at the Sacred Tree of Oneness today. I am grateful for the experience of your presence.

All my relations, all my ancestors, I call to you so that I may honor you within this circle of life at the Sacred Tree of Oneness today. I am grateful for the experience of your presence.

To my Spirit relations who guide me, offer protection in the realms, and carry the torch of Eternal Love, , I call to you so that I may honor you within this circle of life at the Sacred Tree of Oneness today. I am grateful for the experience of your presence.

To my mineral relations that give us the foundation of life experience, , I call to you so that I may honor you within this circle of life at the Sacred Tree of Oneness today. I am grateful for the experience of your presence.

To my plant relations that sustain and heal my body, , I call to you so that I may honor you within this circle of life at the Sacred Tree of Oneness today. I am grateful for the experience of your presence.

To my animal relations that feed my body and offer your guidance in this life, , I call to you so that I may honor you within this circle of life at the Sacred Tree of Oneness today. I am grateful for the experience of your presence.

To my human relations that share my path as we walk upon Mother Earth, , I call to you so that I may honor you within this circle of life at the Sacred Tree of Oneness today. I am grateful for the experience of your presence.

To the Four directions that bring the winds of change and growth, , I call to you so that I may honor you within this circle of life at the Sacred Tree of Oneness today. I am grateful for the experience of your presence.

All my relations within the circle of life that surround the Sacred Tree together as one we celebrate that each may experience the Great Mystery of Oneness.

It is a celebration, a dance that honors the Sacred Tree and the oneness of all life. The energy of our dance is our energy return to the Universe, to all our relations, that have given us the experiences of life. As we dance around the tree our thoughts and our energies ripple out to connect us with all. Each step of our feet upon the ground is sacred and is done with ceremony. It is a pledge to honor all of life.

Take the gift of nourishment (your cornmeal or tobacco gift) and hold it your left hand with your right hand on top as you state your intention of the ceremonial dance. Light your sacred herbs and add

271

the tobacco or cornmeal to the herbs. Honor the 7 directions of the wheel in the manner you have come to use.

Taking the staff which represents Mother Earth, SHE, and begin to dance from East to South to West to North and back to South.

(I used a small staff about 12 inches long and wrapped the end in cotton and leather to also use as a drum beater to assist with beat keeping in the dance).

Keep your feet moving in a side step pattern so that you are looking to the tree the entire time. Your feet should be gentle like they are caressing the Earth. This is not a loud frantic frenzy. This is a quiet reflective dance that may bring you to journey as you move.

You will complete the first round of the East before lifting the sacred herbs once more to each of the 7 directions. You will then begin the second dance round. Your intention and thoughts are upon experiencing the awareness of oneness. You may be joined by dolphins or ancestors as you move through the rounds. You will complete 7 rounds (each direction) before coming to sit before the basket which holds your representation of the spoke you are upon and add to it now in silence the representation of oneness you brought to ceremony.

At this time bring to your thoughts a color, a vibrancies color, whatever comes to you. This is your gift from the Sacred Tree of Oneness to bring to your walk in the mundane. Part of the rainbow energy which will seal your sacred intent.

Awareness of Oneness Sacred Contract

I (add name), having fearlessly walked Center Hub of the East of Oneness, I now make a sacred contract with the Universal Consciousness, the Great Spirit of All.

In the presence of All My Relations, I firmly commit to the following:

1. I will live from my core with impeccability, taking responsibility to act consciously by_____
2. I will step into power and service for the highest good of my community by

   _____
3. I will practice sustainability of all my relations by committing to conserve, recycle and renew by_____
4. I will have reverence for life being interconnected to the web of all and honor daily life as sacred by_____
5. I will honor inclusiveness, diversity and acceptance of all relations and their heritage by _____

6. I will practice collaboration and co creation with others who are in alignment with my soul by _____
7. I will practice the action of gratitude daily by _____

I give myself permission to grow through each step in the living of my vision. Should I fail to honor my own commitment to this Act of Power, I agree to the giveaway of:_____
Sign and Date

Determining your pledge

In reviewing each of the outer spokes, list the spokes in order of strongest to weakest connection with. For example, 1. Winged world, 2. 4 legged world, 3. 2 legged world, etc. The suggestion to me has always been to take the weakest spoke as my pledge and determine one or two things that I can specifically work on to strengthen that spoke and the sacred inter relatedness. Perhaps your weakest spoke is the swimmers. What could you do to work on that spoke; perhaps cleaning water ways? The gratitude giveaway comes from the spoke that is the strongest on your list. Perhaps your strongest is the winged world, what would be something you could give back to the winged world? What about a new feeding home for the winged world perhaps in the form of a bird feeder or adding to your garden for an organic feeding?

The determination of what you need to work on will come from your spiritual accounting and your journals. This accounting will reveal how you can work on strengthening that spoke.

CHAPTER 33

CENTER HUB – SOUTH

HUMAN FAMILY

Virtue:	Responsibility
Intent:	Contemplation
Goal:	Empowerment Accountability
Mantra:	I Walk in Beauty and Balance

The Medicine Wheel walks can provide an integrated, non-linear approach to overall wellbeing spiritually, mentally, physically, and emotionally. As we look to the South and consider our human family and it's inter-relatedness to ourselves, we see the growth into ideals that require us to have courage, personal balance, determination and intentional effort.

When we consider the growth, first we turn to the east first and see the Warrior archetype that requires stamina and leadership. This requires one to stay within their own power and extend honor and respect to others, but it also sees the limits and boundaries that exist. Being present and using right action, right communication, and responsibility. Next we turn to the south and see the Healer archetype that requires us to extend love to ourselves and to others holding both in balance. Seeing the contributions that you have made to the world about you and seeing where it is that you wish to be, one can see what is impeding the soul's progress and focus on what is working. Facing the west we come into the Visionary archetype that calls into question our integrity. Giving voice to what you see both internally and externally through your own actions, intuition, perceptions and insight, yet, knowing the shadow side of being a visionary. The denial and self-indulgence or always seeking approval and love are not part of visionary way of being. Turning to the North where we see the Teacher Archetype that gives the wisdom a voice in clarity, rightness, objectivity and discernment. This is remembering and honoring the ancestors that no longer walk this physical journey and balancing it with the Visionaries that are inspiring; many times needing to return to the Healer self to heal the past before hearing the wisdom.

Each turn looking at self in relationship to our self on the inner spokes, each power as it relates to self is also the relationship with others, the power of others. At times it can be difficult to see the difference between hearing the medicine and comparing the medicine of each.

It is here we look for where our power leaks out or where we give it away and how that impacts the world around us. At times these may be blatant and other times the subtle as they have been a part of our patterns.

Responsibility and Accountability: Empowerment Accounting

Returning to the inner spokes, ask yourself where you hold back from doing your best, where you avoid or deny. What events that involve other humans make you hungry, angry, lonely, tired, or scared? Can you look at your ideal relationship list and identify where your leaks are? When did they begin? How have you acted them out? Balance the spiritual accounting with looking at what brings you the most joy? What is your special beauty in life? What are your strengths? How can you use your strengths more powerfully?

From this list can you identify what actions you can make to empower yourself, within yourself, for yourself? How will these acts of power benefit your family, your community, and all your relations? As you begin to frame this action contract, be sure that you are specific and realistic. Allow yourself to be flexible and know that you can amend it as you change. Make this a gift to you – for you.

278

We have all heard the age old saying, "With great power comes great responsibility". It is even more so when speaking of energetic power. Whatever you gain and/or obtain for power comes with a responsibility that can be a heavy burden to carry. We have spent some time looking at our ethical behaviors, but one side of that we have yet to address is the idea of personal sacrifice. In shamanic terms, and really any service work that comes with great power, comes a need of personal sacrifice. The responsibility of using power is not something undertaken lightly. Many see the power and its use in different facets. Re-connecting with the power that exists in the Universe, re-discovering the power within the spiritual self, and re-learning the responsibility of that power. Why this belaboring upon responsibility and ethics?

Tapping into the void, the mystery, will have an effect upon the lives of those you work with and on. Simply by my writing the words, describing the power, teaching a few basic techniques, I am having a great impact upon your life, my life, and the lives anyone we may all touch in the future. When thought of in this manner, we begin to see the depths of the responsibility and why the insistence on stressing ethics.

We are beginning to see how the work we have done has affected our own life and we certainly can see the possibilities of it affecting the lives of others. Thus we must not only look at our own ethics at this point but the ethics of helping another. The healer, regardless of whether they are an energy healer, shaman, or Reiki Master, has the responsibility and ethical choice of what happens in the work that they do. Even if that work is upon self-verse helping others in the community. I have heard many instances where a healer will say "oh spirit told me to". This is really an excuse for not taking responsibility. The reality is, while Spirit (or any other term you wish to use) does provide the information and they do provide the energy to heal, it is still your duty as the healer as to what will occur and how it will occur. No spirit force comes down to Earth and forces anyone to do anything. The true healer is always an equal partner in the healing process. Equal with spirit – which is why there was so much work upon the ego and ego deflation. One must be willing to listen but also be prepared for the responsibility.

Many of you have done outside work with me and can attest to the fact that I always require a specific permission statement prior to entering another's energy be it for a reading or healing work. Part of that is the responsibility of the work. Imagine this if you will, you are taking this workshop, and you are moving along at the perfect speed for you. Then you hit a stumbling block. Something prevents you from going further. I see this in a journey state. So I step in and remove the obstacle for you because in my mind there should be no negative conation to removing an obstacle. Remember, in this scenario I have not received the personal permission. But I am the teacher, I see the obstacle, I am going to remove it. Yet down the road, when you as the teacher are not around, another obstacle appears – because you robbed them of the experience before which would have allowed them to remove an obstacle with you nearby to guide, they now must figure out how to do it on their own with no guidance. It takes much longer, is more painful, and it could have been avoided.

Let's pause for a moment and look at two different words that are being used here. There is responsibility and accountability. What is the difference? Let me just say this **I take responsibility and I am held accountable**. Hopefully within that simple sentence you can ascertain the difference in meaning for yourself. And while the two words can be interchangeable, that does not mean that they are the same thing. Responsibility is up to you; whereas accountability is up to others.

The second part of this spoke is empowerment.   So for this journey around the center hub we are focused upon self and not others. Answer the following questions from your journey around the inner spokes.

What are the top ten values you have identified as your highest priority (whether you have been able to apply them or not).   Words like achievement, zeal, compassion, passion, as examples.

1.

2.

3.

4.

5.

6.

7.

8.

9.

10.

Now take inventory of where your life is at in this moment regarding these values …. As example: I am in a loving and passionate relationship.
Now look at these values, your inventory or accounting of them, and see if you can determine which of you values are not being met? Which need to be shifted to combine your value and your passion? What needs to shift to make your relationships your optimum relationships?

As you do this for a single relationship, you can go back to this same empowerment exercise and look at your work relationships, your money relationships, your health relationships, or any relationship. The threads you will find will mirror one another whether you are looking at your health, your financial situation or your love life.

The threads of the values in each type of relationship that are frayed or broken will become stronger as you see whether you need to take responsibility for not keeping your own commitment to your values. Taking responsibility empowers your being.

Let's go back to the first part of the spoke. We are going to work further on our mission statement and incorporating our responsibility and empowerment into the statement. To do that we are going use a template which at first may seem a bit strange.

1. What is your greatest ambition? What do you truly love to do, inspires you, or gives you the greatest passion?
2. Now looking at your ambition, why? Why do you want to achieve the ambition? Knowing what your purpose is empowers you. (This is one statement)
3. Looking at the values from the first exercise, how do they align with the ambition and the why answer?
4. As you look at the three pieces in steps 1-3, combining the three will give you are driving purpose in life and your personal mission statement. So structure you mission statement from the three answers. Remember that your statement is a very concise short statement that reveals your ambition for your life based upon your greatest passions and personal values.

- Example: I create (life passion) that (life purpose) and fulfills my desire for (life values).

- I create powerful and profound workshops that inspire and transform people to take responsibility for their own spiritual empowerment and provides me with the financial freedom to offer healing to all who come forth.

So as you create your soul purpose statement here, use the all the notes from your journal exercises to incorporate them into this one exercise. Use the example above to create a powerful statement of your soul purpose. Remember, this is not immovable. It can and will shapeshift as you continue your journey.

Empowerment Sacred Contract

I (add name) having fearlessly walked the Inner Spoke of the South and discovered my soul purpose, I now make a sacred contract with the Universal Consciousness, the Great Spirit of All. In the presence of All My Relations, I firmly commit to the following Act of Power: My Soul Purpose is:

_____

I will take the following actions during the next year to walk the sacred path towards my soul purpose:

a.
b.
c.
d.
e.
f.

I give myself permission to grow through each step in the living of my vision. Should I fail to honor my own commitment to this Act of Power, I agree to the giveaway of:_____
Sign and Date

CHAPTER 34

CENTER HUB – WEST

UNITY

Virtue: Unity

Intent: Balance between masculine and
feminine

Goal: Merging from polarity to unity

Mantra: I am unified with all

When the divine feminine blends with the divine
masculine we come into balance and unity.

Moving to the West Center Hub, I want to share
again as it cannot be over emphasized, there is no
right way nor wrong way to walk the wheel. How
you walk is your choice and it should never be
judged by anyone. There is an ethics principle of
non-interference that comes to mind that teaches it
is not the right of any to place judgment on another
on how they choose to live life. The only right is to
be there in friendship, love, support, and harmony
leaving your personal opinions – personal.

Each and every one of us is created at a perfect soul and that perfection comes together with other perfect souls in unification. Remember that the Great Mystery, the Great Spirit, the Divine does not make mistakes. It was shared with me by a teacher that once upon a time that people would gather in the morning and begins every day in a sacred manner. They would lift up songs and prayers to greet the morning sun and say thank you to the moon. Many times people will ask me why I arise so early at 4 am each day and begin it with meditation and prayer beneath the moon remaining to welcome the sun, it is the tradition that began with this story of morning rising. It is just that a traditional way - not the only way. In this spoke we will look at shadow balance, energy balance, merging all the way to unity within and without.

As we look to the wheel for direction of the unity of human society we realize that you participate in the dynamics of creating your own reality. Your reality and the entire Universal consciousness reality is one in the same. Your participation has an affect now and long after your soul travels into the spiritual realms. Universal reality is created by a group effort and does not simply exist. In order to shift the consciousness of the Universal reality, your soul intention must merge with other soul's to co-create the bands of light frequencies.

The dynamics of the human family is really simply the soul of all human beings. Just as we each individually have a consciousness and a sub consciousness, so does the Universe. This is a merging of the consciousness and sub consciousness of all humans to create the tapestry of the center hub. It is this Universal consciousness that is the collective of all energetic signatures that help the Universe evolve. This hub center is about realizing that you are part of a whole. The whole of the human family is a fluid, flowing, massive co-creative force that exists independently of each soul, yet is interdependent on each soul.

The Universal Human Family has come into creation because as individuals over time we have perceived life in a sense of duality. We believe what we can see, what we can taste, what we can hear, and what we can feel. We as a human family act as though we are not affected when we take from or give to the Universal energetic signature. This is a result of striving for the external power that is truly a destructive competition between human souls. The merging or fusing of sacredness has been lost in the evolutionary process. We have become separated in consciousness.

The Universe that we have created has been done so with unconscious and conscious intentions. Remember that every intention that you have creates an energetic signature whether it is a conscious or unconscious intention. You are co – creating the Universal reality every moment of every day. Every word spoken, every thought that you have, and every emotion you feel carries with it a conscious and unconscious intention that forms and creates a vibrational frequency signature.

When you feel the emotion of anger, even if it is not expressed, you send an anger intention into the Universal consciousness. When you are placed in fear, real or imagined, that fear for survival is sent out as an unconscious energetic signature into the Universe. When you bring the unconsciousness of your soul in alignment with the consciousness of sacredness, you step into your authentic power and begin to co-create a reality that reflects your soul's conscious intention. In this way, what you intend shapes your experience. What you intend becomes your reality.

The difficulty in all this comes in aligning your unconsciousness with your consciousness. It is vital to begin in this hub with bringing the two into unified energetic signatures. It is not enough to affirm your attention. It is not enough to simply
290

pray for your desires. In order to align yourself into unified consciousness, it is necessary to shift your perceptions and beliefs on an unconscious level back into a sacred reverence. If you attend to the shadows, the weakness aspects discovered in the inner spokes, you will begin to shift perceptions and belief patterns. If you ignore and dismiss the shadow aspects you discovered in the inner spokes, you will continue to live in duality and manifest at a lower frequency.

The journey from separation and duality to complete unification begins with each individual soul becoming unified. It is only then that the human family can become unified. It is from a single unified soul's energetic signature that the tribal consciousness will shift. Small bands of tribal light will merge with other tribal bands of light and the shift will begin at the collective level. You start the process when you align your own energetic signature.

Releasing Judgments Exercise

Whether you are reading this as a male (masculine) or female (feminine) most will have internal struggles and judgments about the aspects of masculine and feminine energies. In order to unify the Human Family, one needs to ensure that these judgments have been completely released.

Start with a plain piece of paper and draw a line down the center. On the left label it masculine and on the right feminine. Without thought or perception, just simply allow the answers to flood in. Ask yourself what does feminine energy look like – write simply one to three word answers. Do the same for the masculine energy.

As you look to the lists you created, can you see your judgments playing out?

Remember whatever you judge in self you judge in others and the reverse. Can you see where you are balanced or imbalanced in your own energy?

Now take a second piece of paper and create the same division while answering the questions regarding the human family. What do you perceive society sees as the answers? Think about your familial tribes, your work tribes, and your community tribes.

Shadow Embracing

Returning to the Inner Spokes of the Medicine Wheel where are your shadows? Is there a pattern that emerges? Can you see how the shadows play with the judgment listing created above? What is one shadow aspect that you can identify? How can you work to shift that shadow aspect?

Duality to Unity

In order to move from the separation or duality of energies in the Human Family, we must begin with self. With your lists from above (both the shadow aspects and the attributes), can you identify the aspects of the feminine in which you are missing? The masculine? Can you identify the aspects of the feminine in which you are overdoing them? The masculine?

Here is an example

Feminine   shadow   Masculine
                  shadow
Nurturing   giving more to
others   active   over active
             To balance – self-care, self-
nurture   to balance –pausing,
meditation
Activation Meditation

293

Begin with sitting still, relaxed with your eyes closed. Allow yourself to take a few deep breathes to relax fully.

Visualize two knobs in front of you. One shows an F and the other a M embossed upon them. See yourself reach forward and turn the knob of the M up. As you turn the knob feel the flow of energy through your body beginning on the right side flowing to your fingers and toes before moving to the left side. The energy pulsating. Notice all that you experience. When you are ready, turn the M knob back down.

See yourself reach forward and turn the knob of the F up. As you turn the knob feel the flow of energy through your body beginning on the left side flowing to your fingers and toes before moving to the right side. The energy pulsating. Notice all that you experience. When you are ready, turn the F knob back down.

Take a few deep breaths allow the tingles of energy to settle.

Reach forward with both hands turning each of the knobs slightly until the pulsating energy within feels balanced and blended. Experience the

294

unification of the blending within. Allow yourself to simply experience it.

Knowing the knobs are available for all times, at any time that you may need to call upon additional Divine Feminine Energy or Divine Masculine Energy you can return here effortlessly and easily to adjust your activation knobs.

When you are ready to return, take three deep long breathes and simply flex your wrists and flex your ankles to return feeling refreshed and rejuvenated.

Practice of Unity

Unity is considered or defined by living in harmony with others. True unity celebrates the diversity in the world by finding commonalities between one another, whether it is in action, thought, value, or simply by being a human being. Look at society, your own community, your own workplace – how is it formed? Are their groups divided by economics? Race? Ethnicity? Sexual? Religious? What about gated communities? Politics? There are endless examples of where we practice separation rather than unity. This practice only serves to create a deeper wound that must be healed in order to find unification.

There is a term called the "butterfly effect". This relates to the idea that the small actions taken in one place can result in a large impact in another. The example often used is that a butterfly flapping its wings in the US could have a large impact elsewhere, such as a tornado in China. The theory, in practicality, is truth. What you do energetically has an impact or a ripple effect that is far reaching.

Unity Exercise

Go to where you are using your physical representation of the medicine wheel.

Face the East. See the people of the East. Notice the shape of their eyes and the color of their skin, their clothes, their stance, their expression. What are they saying to you?

Face the South. See and observe the people of the South. What message are they sending to you?

Face the West. See and observe the people of the West. What are they knowing that you need to know?

Face the North. See and observe the people of the North. What are they saying to you?

What did you hear? What messages were shared? Can you see your commonalities with each direction? Can you see what they may offer to you? To the world? What direction do you stand in?

Shadow Aspect Sacred Contract

I (insert name/spirit name) in the presence of the Divine Life Creator and All My Relations, acknowledge my oneness and unity with All Life. I make a sacred contract to reconnect with the Divine Life Creator and All My Relations from the depth of my soul and to give action and beauty to this commitment.

As my sacred act of Unity, I will go to my Sacred Place, make myself open to the teachings, and honor myself and All My Relations in a sacred way.

I pledge to work on the shadow aspect of myself that keeps me in duality identified by walking the spokes of the Medicine Wheel by ____(fill in your shadow aspect and solution)_____.

I give myself permission to grow through each step in the acceptance and acknowledgement of my shadow self. Should I fail to honor my own

commitment to this Act of Power, I agree to the giveaway of: _____
Sign and Date

Remember, it is vital not to set yourself up for failure in this power contracts. The point is to help you become accountable and responsible for your own spiritual accounting. Work on one aspect at a time and know that it is a life time process. Everyone has a shadow or beast within – that shadow or beast serves to keep you balanced. It is only when the shadow/beast self is out of balance that we perceive it to be negative in nature. To bring All Relations into unity – it is vital that we each begin with self-unity. When the individual is in unity, then the tribe can become unified. When the tribe is in unity, then the human society can become unified.

CHAPTER 35

CENTER HUB – NORTH

GREAT FAMILY

Virtue:	Contemplation
Intent:	Inner Divinity
Goal:	Integrity
Mantra:	I walk with sacred integrity and inner Divinity

We return to the North, the Center Hub of the Great Family. The downward spiral connecting the human family with that of all the clans of all the relations from the winged ones to the creepy crawlers; while the upward spiral connects to the Gateway to the Divine Family of the Stars and the Cosmos bringing them into a single moment on the Medicine Wheel. The ancestors among the stars and cosmos have always been the first to be invited to any and all ceremony, it is appropriate that it is here in the north, the winter that the stories of the ancestors are joined with the stories Mother Earth shares. It is here the whispers in the wind can give direction for not only standing at the gateway to the

Spirit World within, our center, but to the gateway to the other worlds in which the Great Family unites.

It is vital to stand here and look to the center where we must be prepared to stand in our raw, naked and vulnerable state. In this naked state all is revealed. Once revealed, it is then we can truly journey to the other worlds. All inter connected and related. It is here at this moment in which we must be clear on what our own spiritual code of ethics are? Allowing at all times the flexibility for new perceptions but steadfast in essence is vital. It is here we must ask ourselves, having defined our ethics, whether we violate our own spiritual codes and why?

It is imperative at this point to understand a few spiritual ideas. Prayer is your connection with the Divine. Meditation is your listening to the Divine. Prayer does not mean going to the Divine with your problems to have the Divine solve them. Prayer means asking for guidance in how to solve the problem yourself. Meditation is listening to that guidance. Prayer is not simply speaking words. Prayer is communion as one with the Divine. To experience the answers one can go further into journey, but one must meditate to hear.

What sort of questions have you sought guidance for in prayer? Do you listen for the answer? Do you not ask because you fear the guidance?

The questions and depths of this hub can go on and on. What are the spiritual ethics that you hold as truth towards the winged ones? Have you violated those codes? What about towards your own power? Or within relationships? Thoughts? What remains to be healed in order to fulfill your own codes? Where are you leaking power as you violate your own codes? Is ego justifying or rationalizing reasons to shift your codes?

Seeking Guidance through Contemplation

As you have begun to notice in this journey walk around the medicine wheel, the directions for journeys, ceremony, and even for the journal work has become less and less. As we prepare to stand as a sage of our own being, our own experience, we no longer follow another's intuition, another's guidance, or even another's steps. It is here that we turn inward toward our own Inner Divinity and ask for the truth. We journey to seek the guidance for our own steps. We listen in meditation to the Divinity who whispers to our soul. It is here that we return to our sacred contracts made and ask ourselves "are we walking with integrity?". Are we

301

following our own sacred contracts to the best of our ability? Are we falling short? What of our code of ethics? Remember, here we are asking from our sage self – the utmost honesty is vital. We all fall short of our ideals, the key is to ask ourselves are we doing our utmost, are we giving life 100%, are we staying within our own integrity?

When we discover those areas that we are falling short, where we have violated our own code of ethics, our own truths, we do not sit and belabor them. Rather we ask for guidance. We ask what steps to take? Do we need shift our own contracts or our own behavior?

As we are preparing for the transition into the Void (or perhaps we are returning to the East of new beginnings), it is imperative that we revisit with a contemplative mindset to our ethics. We work here with the Great Family. This is our connection to the Divinity, our connection to All, and our connection ultimately to our higher self. In the first part of this work we looked to our questions, what are we asking and what are we hearing. Even in the Divinity of life that permeates all things there are choices. Those choices are made based upon our own integrity. Integrity is based upon our ethics.

We have spent a great deal of time review where we stand in life, our thoughts, our values, and our truths. It is here that we go to the Source of All Things and sit with our truths Go back to your ethical statements from Lesson 25. We said as an example I will be honest, especially with myself. I will be forthright. I will be sincere. I will be reliable. This was in relationship to self. Now we ask for the guidance in a raw and vulnerable manner. We ask specifically where we are honest and dishonest, where we are forthright and where are not, where we are sincere and where we are not, and where we are reliable and where we are not to the Great Family. It is here that we have the opportunity to question our contract for this lifetimes walk. It is here that our Divine Team, our Sacred Allies, from the other worlds sits with their records, their expectations, and their judgments. We have the opportunity to ask what the contract of this life is and how we may alter it.

Your Sacred Contract has "choice points" or moments that we are given free will to make choices. These include moments that are directly related to our relationships in life. Relationships are the basis of our learning. They are the dynamics of our energetic contracts. We learn, we heal, and we savor relationships. Yet, we also have the choice point of re-scripting relationships; even the relationships with the great family.

Re-scripting a relationship so that it aligns with your integrity, with your ethical values, is a conscious effort to change the way you interact in life. It can awaken you to new possibilities.

First look at your patterns that have been revealed during your walk. Look back at your ideal relationship description. Does it match your ethical values still? Does your body language change when you read them? Ask yourself if it is a type of person that causes you to abandon your ethics? Does a certain type of relationship pattern cause your tense? Smile? As you discover deeper relationship patterns that cause you to tense and write out once more the way you could shift your reaction to cause peace rather than tense energy.

Relationships clearly reveal to us our true motivations and unconscious beliefs. We must see them simply as patterns if we wish to rescript them.

Many times we will see the victim appear in relationships, blame rears its head. She made me feel--- when she ------. This type of statement is a sign post that we need to shift. Another example, we see another struggling with dieting and we
304

unconsciously taunt them by eating succulent deserts in front of them rather than supporting them. We do this, we think in good humor, but it is really an unconscious need to destroy a relationship.

Ask in your journal:

- What is the most common theme in all your relationships?

- Where are you still experiencing strong emotions of control, jealousy, judgment or criticism?

- Do you find that others are avoiding intimate relationships with you?

- How is your relationship with the material world – money for example?

Take the answers to these base questions to journey, meet with your Divine Team and ask how you might rescript the contract to shift in alignment with your ethics.

Remember that in all things there are four stages of sacred contracts

1. Separation – this is where we want the easy way out – we ask that someone be removed rather than doing the work to shift ourselves. Another way to determine if this is where are "If I find/have ____ then I will be ____ ". This type of statement is always a sign post we are in separation stage.

2. Dark Night of the Soul – this is where you feel lost, ungrounded, and even abandoned. You can't hear or believe in your Divine Team. You believe that you are in crisis. It will come right smack dab in the middle of the most joyous occasion. You suddenly feel catastrophic emotions. Here you want to look closely at your daily spiritual practice. I have found it is rarely what you are doing but rather what you are not doing that leads to this stage. So what have you stopped doing?

3. Light – this is where the light returns. We become joyous once more that the dark has been lifted. Again remember the alchemical lesson. We sometimes stop here because it feels a thousand times better than the dark night. But it is not the end.

4. Appreciation – this is where we want to be. This is the state of humble appreciation for all things. It is the practice of gratitude.

So as you go to your Divine Team to rescript your contract, be sure to know where you are in your journey. Don't ask for things to change if you are not willing to change yourself.

<small>PREPARING FOR THE JOURNEY TO MEET WITH YOUR DIVINE TEAM</small>

With the answers from above and your previous journal entries, write down the specific traits that repeat in your patterns that you wish to shift (your weakness).

Write down the exact trait you wish to shift to. It is best to work with one or two at most for this exercise. Be sure to follow the energy of the trait meaning if you wish to be more patient as you find that one pattern that repeats is your impatience with others to "hear" you. With this trait of patience be prepared to be taught patience. This means that you will have lesson after lesson which will require you to develop this trait. Whatever you ask of your Divine Team in this re-scripting will come to pass in ways you did not expect. Thus, one must be prepared.

Having the trait (or two traits) in mind, go to journey asking your gatekeeper to take you to the hall of Your Divine Team. Speak your truth of
307

what you wish to rescript. I warn you be prepared for some hard criticism, hard truths, to be shown to you. Your Divine Team while they love you for who you are and are on your team, they will be bluntly honest with you. Ask that you be allowed to rescript the trait. Then listen. Listen with your soul not your ears.

As you learn and become adept at re-scripting a single trait you can go to your team and rescript larger parts of your contract. You can negotiate your contract but remember your team can see all and you can only see pieces.

Chapter 36

CENTER – VOID

SPIRIT

Virtue: Harmony

Intent: Mastery of Love Oneness

Goal: Unconditional Love

Mantra: Love One Another In Complete
Oneness

The Great Mystery. The Void. The internal and external Spirit. It is perhaps the greatest questions that exist within the center of the wheel. The Center is a quiet centering within through a deep surrender to All that is. It is the reminder that we are simply a speck of grain carried by the waves of the ocean. It is the tradition now to go into contemplative and reflective meditation / journey. Have we skimped on our walk? Did we ask for guidance and listen? Were we completely honest with self? As we have built a foundation upon which we can build the structure of our lives, did we build upon sand or bedrock?

This is a space that only an individual can know the answers and the questions for themselves. If you find that you have satisfied your inner questions, it is important to close the space for yourself that has been held sacred for this journey around the wheel.

There is a shadow side that must be discussed here. The shadow is death. The death is really about separation. A Separation between self and life, self and Divine, and self and breath. When we enter the center void, there is no destination to describe, no words to explain – it is a vision quest that each must undertake themselves when it is revealed to do so. The question to ask "how is your fire burning". An odd question with a variety of layers to the answer. Is it blazing – a long passionate life. Is it flickering – death near or death of a relationship, are you not speaking your truth.

Whether you are working inward or in the outward expressions of life, the center will inform your life story so that you can become more aware, more connected to the Universe within you.

Many times you will hear the center referred to in this manner:

Upward   Grandfather Sky or Grandmother
Moon
310

	God or Goddess
Downward	Mother Earth
Inward	Spirit within
Lower	Middle world
Interior	Everyday life

Some see it in a more linear manner.

Spirit Guides	Human World	Plant/Animal
Totems		
Angels	Star Beings	Ascended
Masters		

The Andean will call this area of the wheel the center of Ayni which is the sacred reciprocity of life. The Inka will call it Kuchi or the Rainbow Bridge. There are many names, many experiences. Words cannot express it.

We undertake a Vision Quest only when we are prepared for the revelations. It is a rite of passage of sorts, a completion of a cycle, and a turning point in many lives. It is done alone, in silence. It is tradition to spend time fasting and praying before one begins. It is imperative that one has met and worked with their spirit animal who will stand guardian for the quest. Many times a vision quest at this point is a form on an initiation. The sole purpose is to move beyond death and separation. I have seen some undertake a vision quest ill

311

prepared and not returned with solace or sanity. I do not speak this to scare you, but rather to warn you. Do not undertake this lightly. It is better to wait then to rush head strong into a vision quest.

It is also mandatory that before one embarks upon a vision quest that they take the time to purify the body. Whether this is done through a sweat lodge or fasting, it is mandatory.

I know many who see this in some fanciful way of drumming and chanting with others. While there are times that vision quests are done in a group setting under the watchful eye of a medicine man or medicine woman, most vision quests are a time of solitude.

So what is the real purpose? To discover the Great Mystery of life as an experience of unconditional love through a journey to the void.

How does one prepare? All of the work that has been done up to this point through all of the spokes has been leading to the ultimate conclusion. Death. It is death of self. One must be prepared to have the ultimate surrender of all things within to the Great Mystery of Spirit. For most this is a week long process. Three days of fasting and praying. Three days of cleansing and purifying the body, the mind, and the spirit. Offering of herbs and gifts to the spirit world are done during these three days.

This is then followed by a three day quest into the wilderness to be with nature alone. No food or water. No clothing, no tools (except if one happens to be a pipe carrier). Just a blanket. There is no chanting, no drumming – only silence. It is my experience that by the end of day two the visions begin.

After the three days one returns to a day of rest and small sips of water and bits of food. It takes at times 72 hours to fully return to the body. There is always someone who watches over a quester while they are in quest preparation all the way to the return into the body.

I am not going to say a quest is for each of you to undertake, but if you should determine this is for you, please be sure to find a trusted member of your soul tribe or better yet a medicine man or woman to watch over your physical and spiritual body in this realm and all realms. This also gives you someone to share your visions with as they are not to be shared with many.

There is no contract to be written here, it is to be experienced in the quest.

Chapter 37

THE CENTER HUB CONCLUSION

As you have come to the end of your walk around the center hub of the medicine wheel you probably feel wrung out. The process creates dramatic shifts more than the inner spokes, and more than the outer spokes. It is a process that is much like a death of who you are so that you can be reborn to whom you are in truth.

If you have quested or are preparing for a quest, you have surrendered all that you are only to find all that you are within. The center hub is a paradoxical journey. And now ... now you are ready to begin again. It is a constant spiral of going within and spiraling back to begin again. If you remember at the beginning of the journey I shared some believe you begin in the center and spiral outward, while others believe it was as we walked outward towards the center. In either case, it is now time to begin to walk again. Whether you return to the North of the Center Hub with new eyes or you return all the way out to the East of the Outer spokes, we are always beginning again, continuing on, and ending in the same moment.

If you choose to now facilitate others through this process, it is imperative that you follow along with your students. Walk the spokes as you teach them. The more you walk them, the more you question, the more you strive to see with a deeper clarity, the more that will be revealed to you. I can guarantee you that your students will know if you are speaking the words without walking them. They will know if you have visited and revisited the winged world or your own personal code of ethics.

If you have the opportunity to go to a trusted spirit or sweat lodges, take the opportunity to sit in the different directions within the lodge. This will give you an even deeper understanding of the direction.

If you have the opportunity to walk a physical representation of the medicine other than your own, with respect embark upon that journey. Sense the energy, ask to be shown another perspective, another's truth as you walk it. It too will reveal new gifts to you.

Most of all if you should choose to facilitate others through the walk of the spokes, it is imperative that you make the medicine your own,   Don't parrot the beliefs, share your beliefs, share your experiences - make it your medicine.

The sole purpose of surrendering to All is so that you can BE is to become All that you can BE.

Chapter 38

THE JOURNEY CONTINUES

As I shared in the conclusion of the center hub, the journey always continues. Whether you are continuing on your own personal journey or continuing on to share the journey by teaching your own medicine the journey continues.

If you have followed along, answered the questions honestly, and been open minded in your thoughts, you have learned much about yourself and your relationship with all your relations. You have discovered your life purpose and re-evaluated your beliefs. I encourage you to continue to journey the seventh spoke of the inner wheel. It is a lifetime process. I encourage you to keep a journal of your thoughts and emotions. I encourage you to continue to walk the wheel spokes each year and see how it has made shifts in your life.

Many times as you work the spokes of the wheel into your life, it becomes necessary to find a spiritual mentor that you can develop a trust with. In sharing your thoughts, emotions, and beliefs with another person after having completed the journey around the wheel, new insights can be obtained from sharing with a third party. Many religious and spiritual leaders are available for this purpose.

I urge you to continue with the spiral medicine of the wheel and work even deeper with the inter relatedness of All Relations. The outer Circle of Truth reminds us that to gain knowledge for the sake of knowledge will only leave us desiring more knowledge. It is only when knowledge is applied to daily life that the true value is revealed.

Healing through The medicine wheel

Our beliefs anchor themselves in a way that allows for healing to transpire or be blocked. Our beliefs are based upon our spiritual perceptions. When we are looking an anchoring we are speaking of our spiritual family, our community, nature, and the Great Spirit (regardless of the title you choose to bestow upon the Spirit). These connections or anchors are what set up our ability to heal. When we look at our belief's to determine what is whole and healthy, that provides for balance and peace within we can also see those belief structures in our own lives which are fragmented, unhealthy, causing imbalance and discord in our lives. Healing happens when we replace the beliefs that are no longer serving us with ones that are.

Ceremonies such as purification or smudging serve to connect one with their inner divinity, with spirit. They bring awareness into clarity so that one may see their authentic self rather than the victim role of being broken. Other ceremonies are remembrance of what our imprints can be – strong, proud, responsible, and courageous. In remembering, we can then begin to practice these beliefs which serve to heal our minds, our bodies, and our spirits. Healing through the medicine wheel allows one to reconnect the spokes to find the inner balance and peace which is the origin of many physical symptoms.

We have forgotten how to speak our authentic voices and accept our emotions and shifted into a paradigm filled with fear and doubt. When we learn to speak our truths to ourselves and to others we begin to return to a unified being – no longer the lone wolf that is isolated from community. We remember the sacred circle of life. Many times the simple ceremony of silence to listen serves us well, but this must be balanced with ceremony of song to express the inner words. It is through the ceremonial work that we begin to become once more a part of the collective spiritual experience. The collective spiritual experience shifts the perceptions that are the hardest obstacles to overcome. When one is in ceremony with community expressing their authentic voice, learning to balance through the talking stick experience, they begin to experience love, nurturing, and support that comes through community. This joyful experience brings to light the reality of wholeness and unity which alone is not possible. The community ceremony also assists in shifting the belief's around giving and receiving. Seeing a balance in being able to not only support but be supported, not only answer but ask. Our collective experience in the world is how our own perceptions of reality are expressed. So the underlying purpose of ceremony is to express the experience of being within community to establish a deeper connection between self and spirit; as well as between self and community.

The healing continues...

I want you to draw your wheel on paper and mark your directions (E, SE, S, SW, W, NW, N, NE) include your outer, inner, and center spokes. Now with a firm piece of paper (use a manila folders work great) cut out a square (remove the insides so that you have an outline of a square). Take the square and place it on the wheel.

What spokes connect to the four corners? Did you automatically lay it upon the wheel so that the SE, SW, NW, NE connect? What comes up for you when you look at the Inner Spokes of SE, SW, NW, NE? How do they balance one another?

You can repeat this with all shapes. Walk the spoke in a seven pointed star. See how the perspective changes. How about a triangle? It is a never ending journey.

This is the story, the journey. It takes a life time to read, and many lifetimes to understand.

Other Titles Available:

The Illumination

Learn to Heal the Human Energy

Learn to Journey

Learn Psychic Protection

Learn to Write Your Own Affirmations

Learn to Meditate

Learn Power Dressing with Numbers

ABOUT THE CARLA GODDARD, MSC.D., DHP

Carla Goddard, Msc.D., DHP is a contemporary Medicine Woman with a doctorate in Metaphysical Sciences and Clinical Hypnotherapy. She is the founder of Tapestry Living which creates Conscious Living Products. Author of multiple books and 2015 release *"The Illumination"*. She lives in Florida with her husband and three dogs.

Printed in Great Britain
by Amazon.co.uk, Ltd.,
Marston Gate.